D1231392

*Picture on the cover: Marble head of God Helios, measuring 0.55 m. in hight together with the neck, with holes around the hair, where metal rays were fastened. It was found within the wall behind the Inn of Provence, not far from the top of the «Castello» where the ancient Sanctuary of Helios is supposed to have stood. The piece conveys the impression of a centrifugal force about to break out, an effect achieved by the turn of the head in relation to the neck (the effect would probably be accentuated by a similar turn in relation to the body) and by the broad waves of the rich hair. A very characteristic example of hellenistic baroque around the middle of the 2nd century B.C.*

ANCIENT SITES AND SANCTUARIES OF GREECE No 4

Translated by Helen Dalambira
Fotos : Sp. Tsavdaroglou

# CHRISTOS KAROUSOS

LATE DIRECTOR OF THE NATIONAL MUSEUM

# RHODOS

## HISTORY ✺ MONUMENTS ✺ ART

"ESPEROS.. EDITIONS - ATHENS 1973

# HISTORICAL EVENTS AND DATES

B.C.

| | |
|---|---|
| 15th century | : The Mycenaean Greeks (Achaeans) of Argolis occupy Rhodes. |
| 11th century | : The Dorians under Tlepolemos from Tiryns colonize the island; three cities : Ialyssos, Kamiros, Lindos. |
| 700 (approx.) | : Rhodes joins the Dorian "Hexapolis,,. |
| 691/90 | : Lindos throws out colonies to Gela and Phaselis. |
| 6th c. (1st half) | : Kleoboulos, one of the 7 wise men, "tyrant,, in Lindos. |
| 491 | : The Rhodians resist a Persian invasion; Datis besieges — unsuccessfully— the acropolis of Lindos. |
| 480 | : The Rhodians participate with 40 ships in the sea-battle of Salamis, by necessity on the side of the Persians. |
| 478/7 | : Rhodes joins the Athenian League. |
| 464 | : Diagoras of Ialyssos Olympic victor in pugilism; Pindar writes "Olympionikos VII,,. |
| 412/11 | : Diagoride Dorieus (periodonikes) helps the Spartans against the Athenians at the sea-battle of Syme and Rhodes breaks from the Athenian League. |
| 408/7 | : The three ancient cities (Ialyssos, Kamiros, Lindos) "colonize,, the new city of Rhodes, and give it the name of the island. |
| 377 | : Rhodes joins the Second Athenian League. |
| 351 | : Artemisia of Alikarnassos temporarily occupies Rhodes. |
| 342 | : The archaic Kleoboulos' temple of Lindos is destroyed by fire. |
| 316 | : Great flood in the city of Rhodes. |
| 305/4 | : Long siege of Rhodes by Demetrios the Poliorcet (Besieger), terminated by a compromise agreement. |
| 304/292 | : The sculptor Chares works at the famous Colossos of Rhodes. |
| 227/6 | : A destructive earthquake brings about the fall of the Colossos. |
| 190 | : Eudamos, admiral of the Rhodians, defeats Hannibal at the sea-battle of Side (Pamphylia); Hannibal was then advisor to Antiochos III, enemy of the Romans (the "Nike of Samothrace,, may be associated with this event). |
| 167 | : The Romans remove Caria and Lycia from Rhodian administration. |
| 164 | : The Romans sign an "alliance,, with the Rhodians, whereby the latter undertake to recognize the same friends and enemies as Rome. |
| 147 | : The Rhodians help the Romans in the 3rd Carthaginian War. |
| 99 | : The Chronicle of the temple of Lindos is written by Timachidas. |
| 88/63 | : The Rhodians help the Romans in their wars against Mithridates; unsuccessful siege of Rhodes by Mithridates. |
| 42 | : After the assassination of Caesar, Cassius besieges, takes, and severely punishes Rhodes for its failure to help him. Plundering of the sanctuaries of Rhodes. |

A.D.

| | |
|---|---|
| 155 | : Destructive earthquake in "Rhodes; Rhodian oration,, by Ailios Aristeides. |
| 269 | : Rhodes is invaded by the Goths. |
| 297 | : Diocletianus makes Rhodes a part of the "Provincia Insularum,,. |
| 515 | : After the earthquake, the city of Rhodes shrinks into the present area of the Castle. |
| 620 | : The Persians under Hosroes temporarily occupy Rhodes. |
| 653 | : The Saracens under Moabiah plunder Rhodes and remove the bronze of the Colossos (fallen centuries before), which they sell as junk. |
| 807 | : Incursion of the Seltzouks under Aroun al Rashid. |
| 1191 | : Richard the Lion-Heart of England and Philip of France recruit mercenaries in Rhodes. |
| 1204/40 | : Leon Gavalas becomes hereditary "Caesar,, of Rhodes. |
| 1261 | : Rhodes is nominally returned to the Byzantine Emperor but is in fact ruled by the Genoan admirals of Byzantium. |
| 1275 | : The Byzantines repair the walls and the moat of Rhodes. |
| 1306 | : The Genoan admiral Vignolo sells Rhodes, Kos and Leros to the Order of St. John's Knights. |
| 1309/1522 | : Rule of the Knights of St. John; 19 Great Magisters : 1. Foulques de Villaret, 1309-19 (Provence), 2. Hélion de Villeneuve, 1319-46 (Provence), 3. Dieudonné de Gozon, 1346-53 (Provence), 4. Pierre de Corneillan, 1353-6 (Provence), 5. Roger de Pins, 1355 - 65 (Provence), 6. Raymond Bérenger, 1365-73 (Provence), 7. Robert de Juilly, 1373-77 (France), 8. Ferdinand d'Hérédia, 1377-96 (Spain), 9. Philibert de Naillac, 1396-1421 (France), 10. Anton Fluvian, 1421-37 (Spain), 11. Jean Bonpart de Lastic, 1437-54 (Auvergne), 12. Jacques de Milly, 1454-61 (Auvergne), 13. Pier Reymondo Zacosta 1461-67 (Spain), 14. Giovanni Battista degli Orsini, 1467-76 (Italy), 15. Pierre d'Aubusson, 1476-1503 (Auvergne), 16. Emery d'Amboise 1503-12 (France), 17. Guy de Blanchefort, 1512-13 (Auvergne), 18. Fabrizio del Carretto, 1513-21 (Italy), 19. Philippe Villiers de l'Isle-Adam, 1521-2 (France). |
| 1480 | : Unsuccessful but destructive siege of Rhodes by Mohamed II. |
| 1481 | : Severe and very destructive earthquakes. |
| 1498/9 | : Terrible epidemic in Rhodes ("The Epidemic of Rhodes,, by Emmanuel Georgilas). |
| 1522 | : Sultan Souleiman II besieges Rhodes for 6 months. The Knights surrender (December 22) and leave for Malta. |
| 1522/1912 | : Turkish rule in Rhodes. |
| 1912 | : Occupation of Rhodes by the Italians (May 4). |
| 1945 | : Liberation of the Dodecanese. |

*The town of Rhodes, plan (Gabriel).*

# CONTENTS

# KALLIPATEIRA

*"Rhodian noblewoman, how did you enter? An ancient custom bars women from this place.*
*—I have a nephew, Eukles, three brothers, my son and my father, all Olympic victors:*
*you must, oh Hellanodices, allow me a proud place among the beautiful young*
*men competing for Herakles' wild olive branch with admirably manful souls. I am*
*not a woman like the others; my family will shine through the ages with the unwither-*
*ing privileges of brave manhood; it has been glorified by immortal Pindar's golden*
*hymn, written with gold letters on a shining scroll of marble,,.*

L. MAVILIS

The year 408 B.C., one of the last of the Peloponnesian war, was a great year for Rhodes; it was the year in which the Rhodians decided to leave their ancient big cities of Ialyssos, Kamiros, and Lindos, and concentrate in a new and more powerful one. They built this new city at the northeastern corner of the island, and named it Rhodes, like the island.

An important part in this decision and in the new political organization seems to have been played by a Rhodian notable, Dorieus from Ialyssos. He belonged to one of the noblest old families of Rhodes, the Eratid family. Starting with his father, Diagoras, the family had produced a series of renowned athletes. In a period when professionalism in sports was unknown, and most of the competitors were young nobles, a victory at one of the great games was the most striking proof of a man's "virtue,,, i.e. of his overall value and achievement. The amazing victories won by members of this family at all games were so extraordinary, that Diagoras and his descendants, the Diagorides, became famous among the Greeks in their time, and their deeds were taken up and embellished by legends in later generations.

Dorieus himself was a "p e r i o d o n i k e s,,, i.e. a victor in all four Panhellenic Games (Olympic, Isthmic, Nemean, and Pythian). He won victories in the pankratium at three consecutive Olympic Games — 432,428, and 424 B.C. — and was eight times a victor at the Isthmic Games, seven times at the Nemean Games, and a "d u s t l e s s,, victor at the Pythian Games, i.e. he won a victory without so much as dirtying himself with dust, because no one had dared compete with him. His older brother Damagetos was also twice an Olympic victor in the pankration, in 452 and 448 B.C. On the latter occasion, another Olympic victory, in pugilism, was won on the same date by the other brother, Akousilaos.

The two sisters in the family, Kallipateira and Pherenike, had sons who in time became famous pugilists and Olympic victors : they were Eukles and Peisirhodos, respectively. The latter participated in the category of b o y s, which means that he was at the time 17 to 20 years old. As his father had died earlier, his mother Kallipateira (or Pherenike according to others) accompanied him to the stadium disguised in a man's clothes as a coach, for women were forbidden entrance on pain of death. But when her son won —the legend goes— she, in her thoughtless joy, jumped over the fence to run to him, and the garment parted and revealed her sex. The judges, however, forgave her and let her live, considering that she was mother, daughter, sister or aunt of six Olympic victors.

Diagoras, the father, was himself a famous man. Nearly 2 m. tall (Pindar calls him "e n o r m o u s,,), he was also a "p e r i o d o n i k e s,, having repeatedly won at all four great Panhellenic Games and at many others. When his sons Damagetos and Akousilaos won the pankration and pugilism competitions on the same day, in 448 B.C. in Olympia, the father was among the spectators. The sons carried him around the stadium while the crowd showered flowers upon him in adulation for his unprecedented happiness. It was on that occasion that a Lacedaemonian is reputed to have shouted to him : "Die, Diagoras, for you cannot go to Olympos,,, meaning that since he could not become a god, there could be no greater happiness in store for him if he survived this moment of supreme bliss.

The statues dedicated by these 6 Rhodians to Olympia kept their glory alive for many centuries, at least down to the time of Pausanias (2nd century A.D.), but excavations brought to light only some fragments of the inscriptions on their bases. Diagoras the father, however, ensured himself a far more lasting monument, when he had a no lesser man than the great Pindar to write him a "hymn,, for his Olympic victory in 464 B.C. Pindar's "Olympionikos VII,, is not only one of Pindar's best, but also a great tribute to Rhodes for in order to do the athlete an honour commensurate with the glory of his victory, Pindar chose to tell in his poem of all the glorious past of Rhodes. After an exquisite preamble which echoes the joyful solemnity of a wedding ceremony, the poet praises Rhodes, the sea-born daughter of Aphrodite and the bride of the Sun, by referring to the old legends in tones which are reminiscent of the "raises of the bride,, in our folk songs; in the strongly plastic and physical imagination of the ancients, the lovely island could not, indeed, fail to be identified with a nymph (the word in Greek is synonymous with "bride,,) of the same name — the nymph "Rhodo,, as the poet Gryparis calls her. She is the personification of Rhodes, and her loveliness is the loveliness of the island. Pindar relates the three main legends connected with the island's history, starting from the most recent and going back to the most remote, with details which make them throb with life : he tells of how the

Sun-god first made the island and the "nymph,, his own; of the gifts bequeathed to the islanders —his descendants— by Zeus and Athene when she
was born; and of the colonization of the island by the Dorians of Argos.

So beautiful a hymn written by so great a poet about the island and its
inhabitants, was naturally a source of pride not only to Diagoras and his
family but for all Rhodians; a historian of the 2nd century B.C. reported
that it was written with golden letters on a pillar of marble, and kept in the
famous sanctuary of Athene in Lindos — a detail recalled by Mavilis in the
sonnet quoted above.

# THE ODE OF PINDAR VII

## FOR DIAGORAS OF RHODES

Even as when one taketh up in his wealthy hand
a golden bowl, the prime of his possessions, a bowl
that foameth with the dew of the vine, and giveth
it to the youth, whom, when betrothed unto his
daughter, with a friendly draught he welcometh from
one home to another, for the sake of them that sit
at drink with him, and in honour of his new alliance;
and thereby, in the presence of his friends, maketh
him envied for this union of true love. Even so,
while I am sending to the men who win the prize
my liquid nectar, the Muses' gift, the sweet fruit of
my fancy, I pay homage to them, as victors at
Olympia and at Pytho. Blessed is he who is ever
encompassed by good report; but the Grace that
giveth life its bloom looketh with favour, now on one,
now on another, not only often with the sweetly-
sounding lyre, but also amid the varied notes of the
flute.

And now, to the music of both, have I come with
Diagoras to land, while singing of the daughter of the

sea, the child of Aphroditê the bride of the Sun,
even Rhodes; that so I may honour, for his fairness
in fight and his skill in boxing, that giant form which
won the crown beside the Alpheüs and the stream of
Castalia, and also his father Dâmâgêtus, in that he
was well-pleasing unto Justice, while both of them
are dwelling amid Argive spearmen in the isle of
cities three, near the foreland of broad Asia.

Full fain shall I be to proclaim my message, and
duly to tell my tale that toucheth all the common
stock descended of old from Tlêpolemus, even the
widely powerful race of Heracles. For, on the
father's side, they boast  descent from Zeus, while, on
the mother's, they are sprung from Amyntor, through
Astydameia, his daughter. But countless are the
snares that hang around the minds of men, and there
is no means of finding what is best for a man to light
on, not only now, but also in the end. For, on a day
in Tiryns, Tlêpolemus, the founder of this land, struck
with his staff of hard-grained olive-wood Licymnius,
the bastard brother  of Alcmênê, on his coming
forth from the chamber of (his mother) Midea.
Tumult of mind hath ere now caused even the wise
man to go astray. Therefore Tlêpolemus went to
the god of Delphi and asked of the oracle.

Then the Lord of the golden hair spake from the
fragrant shrine of his temple, and bade him sail with
his ships, straight from the shore of Lerna to the sea-
washed pasture-land, where, in olden time, the great
King of the gods shed on a city a snow - shower of
gold, what time, by the cunning craft of Hephaestus,
at the stroke of the brazen hatchet, Athênê leapt
forth upon the crest of her father's head, and cried
aloud with a mighty shout, while Heaven and Mother
Earth trembled before her.

Then it was that the god that bringeth light unto
men, even Hyperîon, enjoined his dear children
to give heed to the rite that was soon to be due,
how that they should be the first to build for the
goddess an altar in sight of all men, and, by
founding a holy sacrifice, gladden the heart of the
Father, and of the Daughter with the sounding
spear. Now it is Reverence, daughter of Fore-
thought, that implanteth in men high merit and its
attendant joys. Howbeit, a strange cloud of forget-
fulness draweth near them in baffling wise, and
causeth the path of duty to vanish from the mind.

For, when they climbed to the height, the seed of
blazing fire had been forgotten; and thus it was
with fireless sacrifices that, on the citadel, they laid
out the sacred precinct. He caused a yellow cloud
to draw nigh to them and rained on them abundant
gold, while the grey-eyed goddess herself bestowed
upon them every art, so that they surpassed all
mortal men by their deftness of hand, and along the
roads rose works of art like unto beings that lived
and moved; and great was their fame. Yet, to
the wise man, even surpassing art is no magic
power.

But the tale is told in ancient story that, when
Zeus and the immortals were dividing the earth
among them, the isle of Rhodes was not yet to be
seen in the open main, but was hidden in the briny
depths of the sea; and that, as the Sun-god was
absent, no one put forth a lot on his behalf, and so
they left him without any allotment of land, though
the god himself was pure from blame. But when
that god made mention of it, Zeus was about to order
a new casting of the lot, but the Sun-god would
not suffer it. For, as he said, he could see a plot
of land rising from the bottom of the foaming main,
a plot that was destined to prove rich in substance
for men, and kindly for pasture; and he urged that
Lachesis of the golden snood should forthwith lift up
her hands and take, not in vain, the great oath of the
gods, but consent with the Son of Cronus, that that
island, when it had risen forth into the light of day,
should for ever after be a boon granted to himself
alone. And all these several words were fulfilled
and fell out truly. From the waters of the sea arose
an island, which is held by the Father of the piercing
beams of light, the ruler of the steeds whose breath
is fire. There it was that the Sun-god was wedded
of old with the nymph of the isle, and begat seven
sons, who inherited from him minds wiser than any

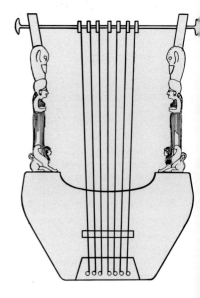

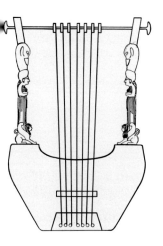

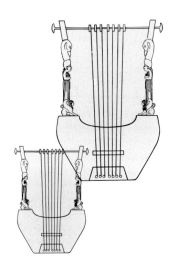

among the heroes of olden days; and, of these, one begat Cameirus, and Ialŷsus, the eldest born, and Lindus; and, with the land of their sire divided into three shares, they had their several cities apart from one another, and their dwelling - places were called after their own names.

There it is that, in sweet requital for that sad mischance, there is still established for Tlêpolemus, the chief of the Tirynthians, even as for a god, a reeking sacrifice of flocks that pass in procession, and a contest of the games.

With flowers from that contest, twice hath Diagoras crowned himself, and at the famous Isthmus four times, in his good fortune; and, again and again, at Nemea and at rocky Athens; while he is not unknown to the shield of bronze in Argos, and the works of art given as prizes in Arcadia and at Thebes, and to the duly ordered contests amid the Boeotians, and to Pellana, and to Aegina, where he was six times victor, while in Megara the reckoning on the tablet of stone telleth no other tale.

But do thou, O father Zeus, that rulest over the height of Atabyrium, grant honour to the hymn ordained in praise of an Olympian victor, and to the hero who hath found fame for his prowess as a boxer; and do thou give him grace and reverence in the eyes of citizens and of strangers too. For he goeth in a straight course along a path that hateth insolence; he hath learnt full well all the lessons, prompted by the prudence which he inheriteth from goodly ancestors. Suffer not the common glory of the seed of Callianax to be buried in obscurity. Whenever the Eratidae are victorious, the city also holdeth festivities; but, in one single space of apportioned time, the breezes swiftly change from day to day.

# HISTORY

**Mythical years**

In the minds of the ancient Greeks, not only in the early period but well into the Classical Era, a "myth,, was no different from a true story. A "myth,, was a thing told, a narrative, a tale passed down by word of mouth, whose origin no one remembered, but which was believed to be true —a "myth,, had not yet been equated to a made up story. The Greeks in fact were convinced that the historical events of their own, as well as of earlier times, were the logical consequence and the continuation in time of the occurrences narrated in the myths. Putting aside the legendary and poetical element inherent in any tale of the early period, we often find that hardly any important historical event was ever completely lost from memory without leaving traces, in those ancient myths.

When the Rhodians listened to their local myths in Pindar's hymn, they had no doubt that this was the true ancient history of their island. The mythical information about that period is now supplemented by archaeological findings and place names. The latter sometimes take us even further back than archaeological evidence. Most place names are pre-hellenic i.e. created by people who were not Greeks but related to the populations of Asia Minor (Caria, Lycia, Lydia, etc.), and many of them have come down through the ages unchanged. Such are, for instance, the names of Ialyssos, Kamiros, Lindos, Ladarma (now Alaerma), Loryma (a Carian name), Atabyris or Atabyrion (a Lydian name) perhaps even Rhodes, which is supposed to be derived from "rhodon,, ( = rose), a non-Greek word.

This mythical complex includes the myths later told by the Greeks of the historical period of Rhodes about the early inhabitants, prior to the colonization of the island by the Dorians; for anything in these myths that can be regarded as a blurred remembrance of actual historical events must be a reference to that Prehistoric Period and most probably to those prehellenic tribes whose idiom was akin to the languages of Asia Minor. Such ancient tribes mentioned in the old myths include the A u t o c h t h o n s or I g n e t e s ( = natives), the H e l i a d e s, direct descendants of Helios —the Sun— variously described as leaders of the Autochthons or as a differ-

ent tribe, and above all the T e l c h i n e s, a strange race of men or "demons,, surrounded in the myths by an aura of admiration mingled with fear. Etymologically, the name was derived by the Greeks from the verb "thelgein,, ( = to charm), so the Telchines were the "Charmers,,, and indeed the myths are full of the tales of their "charms,, and wizardry. A fact attesting to their prehellenic origin is that the myths associate them with deities earlier than the Olympian gods, e.g. with Kronos, for whom the Telchines made the "harpe,, wherewith he maimed his father, Uranos (the "harpe,, was a sickle-shaped sword, the typical weapon of the inhabitants of southwestern Asia Minor, which must have been the terror of the early Rhodians); with Rea, who gave them the young Poseidon to rear; also with the cult of Zeus on Mt. Atabyrion, and with the worship of the Lycian Apollo. They were, we are told, wicked in their souls and repulsive in their appearance. They had the power to conjure bad weather and storms. Above all, however, they were excellent sailors (amphibian) and skilled craftsmen, particularly statue-makers and metal workers. The Chronicle of the Lindos temple, written by the local historian Timachidas around 100 B.C., mentions a crater offered by the Telchines to the Lindian Athene, which "no one could tell what it was made of,,. Their excellent craftsmanship, however, was nothing but wizardry, and it is this "phoniness,, that Pindar hints at when he exalts the "art with no magic power,, of the Greek craftsmen of historical Rhodes who had been taught by no lesser a master that Athene herself. When eventually the time came for the Telchines to leave the island, they sprayed it out of sheer malice with the disastrous water of the Styx, laying the land waste for a long time thereafter.

Archaeological findings up to-date do not go back to very ancient times. No neolithic settlements have been found, though neolithic tools do come up now and again in Lindos; but these findings may be accidental, since important neolithic settlements have been located in Kos and Kalymnos. However that may be, the fact is that abundant evidence of life and civilization on the island begins only with the Late Bronze Age, the so-called Mycenaean Period (from 1500 B.C. on), represented by the rich cemeteries of Kamiros and Ialyssos. The pottery found in these tombs is Mycenaean, identical with the famous potteries of Argolis and of the rest of the Greek mainland

and have been dated by means of Egyptian scarabees. It would seem, then, that in the 15th century B.C. the Mycenaean Greeks of Argolis and the vicinity, i.e. the pre-Dorian Achaeans, after conquering Crete, proceeded east all the way to the coast of Lycia, Pamphylia and Cilicia, taking in the islands including Rhodes in their progress; it is from them that the acropolis of Ialyssos retained the name of Achaïa down to historical times.

### Dorian Colonization and Archaic Era

Only a few centuries later, the Dorian migration which according to the ancient tradition occurred 80 years after the Trojan War (Trojan War, 1184 B.C.; campaign of the Herakleides 1104), once again caused a great upheaval on the mainland of Greece; the new Greek immigrants, the Dorians (or Herakleides), follow upon the footsteps of their predecessors, the Achaeans, and come to Rhodes. Their leader is probably Tlepolemos of Tiryns. The Iliad has it that he was the son of Herakles (Hercules) and that he had had to flee from his home after killing his father's uncle, the old Likymnios, and came to Rhodes with a host. These Dorians divided the island into three sectors under the cities of Lindos, Ialyssos, and the "whitish,, (a r g i n o e n t a) Kameiron, respectively. They did well, for Zeus who came to love them exceedingly, heaped riches upon them, as Pindar's Hymn will point out later. Tlepolemos participated in the Trojan War with 9 ships of the "polytimemenoi,, (a r - r o g a n t) Rhodians; but he was fated not to return. During the famous battle in which Diomedes proved his prowess (Il. E), "the son and the grand-son of Zeus,, found themselves facing each other, and the son, Sarpedon, an ally of the Trojans, killed Tlepolemos, the son of Herakles. Sarpedon was the leader of the Lycians of Asia Minor, and according to one tradition, the founder of the Ionian Miletus. So this legend of the conflict between the Dorian Tlepolemos and Sarpedon from Asia Minor may in fact be a symbolic reference to actual fighting between the Dorians of Rhodes who were attempting to spread over to the opposite coast across the sea and then proceed to the north, and the Ionians of Miletus who were trying to expand in the opposite direction.

Whether that is true or not, at the dawn of the Historical Period of Greece which begins with the arrival of the Herakleides, the Dorians are established in Rhodes. When the Ionian League (Panionion) was established around 700 B.C. with the sanctuary of the Helikonian Poseidon at Mykale as its religious centre, the Dorians responded by forming the "Hexapolis,, (six-city alliance) which included Lindos, Ialyssos, Kamiros, Kos, Knidos and Alikarnassos (the latter severed itself later) and its religious centre was the sanctuary of Apollo at Cape Triopion in the Knidian peninsula. It is therefore evident that "Dorianization,, not only of Rhodes but of all nearby islands had been completed long before : the language, the customs, the political organization, the religious rites, all were Dorian. The same features can be identified in the first certain Rhodian colonies, created in that early period by the population surplus of the island.

Ancient tradition tells us that in 691/690 B.C. the inhabitants of Lindos sent out two colonies at the same time : one to the west and one to the east under two brothers as their respective leaders. The former became Gela on the southwestern coast of Sicily, built by the Lindians together with a number of Cretans, the colony leaders being Antiphemos of Lindos and Entimos from Crete. The second colony was led in the same year by Antiphemos' brother, Lakios, to the coast of Pamphylia, where they built Phaselis. Both colonies retained for a long time their Rhodian character and their devotion to the deity of their fathers, the Lindian Athene.

The island owed its prosperity to trade, i.e. to its favourable position on the seaways between east and west, north and south. The main east-west trade route since times immemorial started from Argolis, Aegina, Megara, or from as far away as Sicily, and proceeded via the Cyclades and Rhodes to Cyprus and Syria. No less important was for the Rhodians, then as later under the Ptolemies, the trade route to E-gypt; this started from the Ionian coast of Asia Minor (Miletus or farther up the shore), met the east-west trade route at Rhodes, headed straight down to the Nile delta, and then turned west to Cyrene. As early as the Archaic Period, Rhodes maintained constant relations with the rulers of Egypt; the sequence of these relations is demonstrated by : a scarabee of Psammitichus I (664-610 B.C.) found in a tomb in Kamiros; mercenaries from Ialyssos going with other Greeks to help Psammitichus II (594-589) in his war against the Ethiopians, and going up the Nile as far as Elephantine of Nubia (Abu-Sibel); the choice position accorded to the Rhodians by Amasis (570-526 B.C.) at Naukratis, the new Greek trade centre on the Nile, and the valuable gifts he sent to the Lindian Athene.

Further evidence of the island's prosperity is the fact that Kamiros as early as the 6th century, and Lindos, and Ialyssos from the 5th century on, each minted her own coins.

The island's main personality in those years was the Lindian Kleoboulos, son of Evagoras, a man of ancient royal blood and a contemporary of Solon. His political activity was naturally restricted to his home city, Lindos, where, as tradition has it, he was a "tyrant,, for 40 years. He became famous all over Greece as a temperate and wise ruler and he was included among the seven wise men of antiquity. He wrote "songs,, and "puzzles,,, and even the well-known "swallow-song,, sung by the children of Lindos as a greeting to spring, has been attributed to him.

## Classical Period. Synoecism

The Rhodians do not seem to have participated in the Ionian uprising (499-494 B.C.), which marked the beginning of the Persian Wars. They did, however, offer resistance to the Persian General Datis sent by Darius with a numerous army and a large fleet to subdue Greece in 491/90. The Persian fleet first called at Rhodes, and in terror the inhabitants withdrew into the "fortifications,,, mostly into the acropolis of Lindos, where Datis besieged them for a long time; but, as we are informed by the Lindian Chronicle, the goddess Athene saved them by a miracle: hard-pressed by lack of water —so the story goes— they were planning to surrender when Athene came in a dream to one of the rulers and advised him to hold on, as she was going to ask her father, Zeus, to provide the badly needed water. The besieged counted their remaining water reserves and proposed to Datis to deliver the city to him within five days, if Zeus did not send the promised help. Datis laughed, but on the following day, one huge black cloud gathered over the acropolis, and then burst sending large amounts of water into the stronghold. The barbarians were filled with fear, as it became obvious that "these men are guarded by the gods,,. They concluded a peace and left, but only after Datis had dedicated many valuable gifts to the temple of Athene.

At the sea-battle of Salamis (480 B.C.), the Rhodians fought with 40 ships on the side of the Persians against the Greeks, as did many Dorians and Ionians of the Aegean Sea. Later, however, after the Persians had been definitely defeated and Aristides founded the Athenian League in 478/7, the Rhodians joined the League by paying the required taxes.

On the whole, Rhodes remained loyal to the League, though the old aristocracy of the Dorian island could not be happy with the democratic spirit which was being radiated by it. We had occasion earlier to mention one of these ancient houses of Ialyssos, the family of the Eratides, from which came the famous victors at the Panhellenic Games —the Diagoras glorified by Pindar and his sons Damagetos, Akousilaos, and Dorieus. Dorieus sided openly with Sparta during the Peloponnesian War (431-404 B.C.) The Athenians sentenced him to death (425 B.C.) and Dorieus had to flee from Rhodes and settle at Thuria in Lower Italy. This naturally did not make him a friend of Athens, and when later the Sicilian disaster (414 B.C.) had weakened the Athenian might, Dorieus with ten ships helped the fleet of Sparta destroy the Athenian fleet off Syme (412-411 B.C.). Shortly after that, Spartans and Dorieus' Rhodians together landed at Rhodes and persuaded the inhabitants to break with Athens. Measures were immediately initiated to effect the union of the three cities under an aristocratic regime. Three years later, in 408 B.C., the great event of the Synoecism of the three cities was consummated, and the population was —partially— resettled in the new city, Rhodes, at the northeastern promontory where it still stands.

In the new state organization whose official name was "D a m o s  R h o- d i o n,, (city of the Rhodians), the three old town communities were maintained but there was now one common  E c c l e s i a  (popular assembly) which met at the city of Rhodes and a  B o u l e  (Parliament). The Parliament changed every 6 months, as did the "p r y t a n e i s,, (rectors), in whom the executive was vested. The supreme ruler in each year was the high priest of Helios (the Sun) for that year. For internal matters, however, each of the three old towns had its own local parliament, composed of the "m a s t r o i,,. The social character of the Rhodian state was later aptly defined by Strabo as follows : "The Rhodians care for the people although they are not ruled by the people, but they want to hold back the crowds of the poor. So the people have their wheat assured, and by an ancient custom, the well-to-do support the needy,,.

One year later, in 407 B.C., the Athenians captured Dorieus; but even though they had condemned him to death many years before, they took pity on him and released him without even receiving ransom. His kin in Rhodes, the Diagorians, were pro-oligarchy and pro-Sparta. But Dorieus no longer shared their views and tried to get his city out of the Spartan League, and this actually happened in 396/5 B.C. But the Spartans succeeded in capturing him, and then something happened which is characteristic of the difference between a democracy and an oligarchy : though the Athenians had spared his life, the Spartans put to death this thrice Olympic victor in his old age.

The early years of the 4th century was a turbulent period for the young state, and power frequently passed from the oligarchic to the democratic party, from the pro-Spartan to the pro-Athenian faction, and vice versa. In 377, the Athenian League was revived and Rhodes again joined the Athenians. But toward the middle of the century, their independence was seriously threatened by the satrap of Caria, Mausolus (the Mausolus associated with the famous "Mausoleum„ of Alikarnassos); in an attempt to expand his sphere of rule, Mausolus attempted to detach the Rhodians from the Athenian League and to have his own appointed people assume political power; his wife and heir Artemisia succeeded indeed in capturing the Rhodian fleet, whereupon she forced an entrance into the city, put the aldermen to death and even set up a bronze trophy.

In the later part of the 4th century, historical developments are dominated by the wars of Philip II (359-336) and Alexander the Great (336-323). first against the Greeks and later against the Persians. Two Rhodian brothers, typical adventurous mercenary leaders (condottieri) render great services to the Persian king against the Macedonians. On the whole, however, the Rhodian state, caught as it were between the warring powers, tried to adopt the policy most favourable to its trade. When it became evident that Alexander was the winner, they sided with him and Alexander reserved them a friendly welcome.

## The Hellenistic Period and the Prime of Rhodes

The destruction of Tyrus in 332 B.C. and more particularly the creation of Alexandria in 331 were events of far-reaching importance for Rhodes, who had always been jealous of her trade interests in the land of the Nile. There is evidence that the political structure of Alexandria was modeled on that of Rhodes; a small island off the port of Alexandria was named "Antir-rhodes„ "as if it were competing with Rhodes„, said Strabo. Rhodian traders fetched wheat from Egypt and supplied it mainly with wine, as evidenced by the great number of Rhodian seals on wine jugs, found there. And, as reported by Diodoros, "it so happened that they obtained the largest part of the profits of tradesmen sailing to Egypt, and that that country was provided almost entirely by them„.

Therefore, when, after the death of Alexander the Great (323 B.C.) his successors quarrelled among themselves, and Antigonos (the One-Eyed) in 307/6 called upon the Rhodians to ally themselves to him in the war against the King of Egypt Ptolemy I (Soter), the Rhodians refused. Their refusal brought about one of the longest but also one of the most glorious adventures in their history: the famous siege of Rhodes (305/4 B.C.) by the son of Antigonos, Demetrios the Poliorcet (Besieger), a man famed for his prowess and his strategic talent.

Diodoros tells of the dramatic incidents of that siege. For a whole year, Demetrios tried in vain to capture the city, by striking now at her ports, now at her walls on the land; he put to work the most sophisticated siege machines —machines whose ingenuousness is admired by experts— but to no avail. The Rhodians resisted with all their resources; the rich contributed their money and the numerous renowned craftsmen their skill. By dint of determination and inventiveness (they even devised a sort of small fireboats) they thwarted all of Demetrios' attempts; they also received help from Demetrios' enemies, especially Ptolemy. Finally, by the mediation of several Greek cities and at the urgent recommendation of Antigonos and Ptolemy, Demetrios and the Rhodians came to an agreement, whose terms guaranteed the Rhodians' independence and honour. Encouraged by their success and proud of it, the Rhodians set up many considerable offerings to their gods, including the famous Colossos of Helios, the work of the Lindian Chares, a pupil of Lysippos.

Throughout the 3rd century and the disturbances caused by the clash of the conflicting forces of Pyrrhos, the Kings of Macedonia, the Ptolemies, the Seleukides, the Romans, etc., Rhodes adhered to her traditional prudent policy, directed mainly at the preservation of her commercial interests; under the right circumstances, she would side with one of the combattants; at other times she would offer to act as mediator. Her prosperity, and hence her political and military power kept increasing; the Rhodian state was able to offer financial assistance to other Greek cities or private Greek citizens. As a result, her moral image was also very high. Thus, when in the year 227 or 226 B.C. a violent earthquake (the same that shattered the famous Colossos) destroyed a large part of the city, of the walls and the shipyards, the Rhodians were readily offered help by nearly all heads of state, many of whom were at war among themselves, When, in 220 B.C., Byzantium attempted to impose a levy on all merchandise leaving the Black Sea, all commercial states affected by the levy authorized the Rhodians to handle the situation with full discretionary powers, "because they considered the Rhodians as dominant over the sea - trade,, they declared war on Byzantium and had the tax abolished.

From the last decades of the 3rd century on, the ever bolder interference of Rome with Greek and Near Eastern affairs, forced Rhodes to decide upon a policy towards this emerging new power. Bent on profiting by the new constellation of forces, it adopted an almost friendly attitude towards Rome. More —she came by degrees to regard Rome's enemies as her own, and so she treated Philip V of Macedonia (221-179 B.C.) as well as Antiochos III (the Great) of Syria (223-187) as her own enemies. In the latter's war with the Romans, which ended up with his destruction at Magnesia, the Rhodians fought against him, and their admiral, Eudamos, defeated the great ancient enemy of the Romans and now military advisor to Antiochos, Hannibal at the sea-battle of Side in Pamphylia (190 B.C.) In the early decades of the

2nd century, the island enjoys the peak of its material and moral ascendancy; the Rhodian fleet is extremely powerful. Rhodes was freed from Macedonian rule and has assumed the protection, almost the hegemony, of the Community of Islands (the Cyclades), the centre of which was Tenos or Delos. But neither this privileged position of Rhodes nor the gratitude of the Romans were to last long.

Under the agreement between the Romans and Antiochos, Caria and Lycia had been given to Rhodes but the Lycians, from the very beginning, had endeavoured to regain their independence. This led them frequently to complain to the Roman Senate against the Rhodians, and finally the Senate openly sided with them, mainly in retaliation for the Rhodians' reluctance to side with the Romans in the conflict with Perseus (178 - 167 B.C.), who had succeeded Philip V. When, in 168 B.C., Perseus was defeated at Pydna by the Roman general L. Emilius Paulus, a Rhodian delegation which had previously gone to Rome to mediate between the two opponents, was forced to congratulate the Senate. The Romans, however, showed them no favour, and even decided to "teach the Rhodians a lesson,,; they asked them in fact to put to death those of their compatriots who, by word or deed, had expressed their favour to Perseus. One praetor even suggested that Rome declare war against Rhodes but that was prevented by Cato. The Romans did retaliate, however, by taking away most of Caria and Lycia and making them independent in 167 B.C., and —what was more— by declaring Delos a free port and giving her to the Athenians in 166 B.C. This was a lethal stroke to Rhodian trade. The proceeds from the port of Delos had amounted in the few previous years to 1,000,000 Rhodian drachmas which, at a tax rate of 2 %, represented 50,000,000 drachmas' worth of merchandise moving through the port. Now this income abruptly fell to 150,000. It is said that the Rhodians then remembered Hannibal who, following his defeat at the seabattle of Side by the Rhodian admiral Eudamos had written a book about the Romans' actions in Asia after the agreement with Antiochos, dedicating it to the Rhodians by way of showing them what they might expect from Roman friendship.

From then on, the island's history essentially followed the political and military adventures of Rome. In 164 B.C., the Romans finally condescended to conclude with the Rhodians an alliance, which required the latter to have the same friends and enemies as Rome. The Rhodians faithfully kept their promise, though they suffered a great deal from Rome's enemies. The greatest disasters, however, fell upon them whenever the Romans had one of their civil wars. The Rhodians did not know which side to choose, since each party claimed to be the legitimate one, and neither would allow the Rhodians to remain neutral.

During the 3rd Carthaginian war, in 147 B.C., they helped Scipio Emilianus (Africanus the Younger) with a fleet, in which served, incidentally, a famous Rhodian, the great stoic philosopher Panaetios. The destruction of Carthago in 146 B.C. and of Corinth in the same year (by Mommius) was of some advantage to the Rhodians since both these cities were its competitors in trade, but, on the other hand, the large wine exports to Carthago stopped forever.

Also in the long and destructive Mithridatic wars (88-63 B.C.), Rhodes remained loyal to Rome, though it had previously had good relations with the King of Pontus, Mithridates VI (Eupator), in whose honour it had indeed set up a statue in the most prominent part of the city. During the war, which began with a terrible mass slaughter of the Romans of Asia Minor, those who managed to survive and escape, sought refuge in loyal Rhodes. Mithridates besieged Rhodes for many months but proved unable to conquer it. The Rhodians finally helped the Romans, at great material sacrifice to themselves, in the war with Mithridates' dangerous allies, the sea-robbers, until the war ended with the brilliant victories of Pompey (67-63 B.C.).

Not long after, however, civil war broke out between Pompey and Julius Caesar. The famous Cato (the younger) persuaded the Rhodians to side with Pompey. At the battle of Pharsala (48 B.C.) where Pompey was defeated, the Rhodians had fought on his side. Julius Caesar, however, forgave them and renewed the alliance. But for that, too, the Rhodians had to pay dearly. In 44 B.C., the democrats of Rome assassinated the Caesar who planned to become a monarch. The two leaders of the conspiracy, Cassius and Brutus, went to Asia Minor to fight the Caesar's friends. Cassius, the more violent of the two, who had been educated in Rhodes, demanded overt and generous help of the Rhodians. When they tried to evade his demand by making their help dependent on the Senate's decision, Cassius besieged. Rhodes, conquered it and dealt cruel punishment by killing many of its inhabitants and imposing very heavy fines, he took away their ships and removed all gold and silver from the temples as well as from private houses. Rome was soon a storehouse of Rhodian works of art. "He left the Rhodians nothing but the Sun,, (the famous chariot with the Sun, Lysippos' work). Finally in 42 B.C., Octavian (the subsequent Augustus) and Antonius, defeated Brutus and Cassius at Philippi, and both conspirators committed suicide Thus Rhodes was theoretically avenged. In the sanctuaries of the island, festivities were organized to "celebrate the end of the war,, and all believed that "peace and prosperity had come,,. In truth, peace and prosperity for Rhodes, as well as for the rest of Greece, would depend on the situation of the Roman state.

The efforts extended by all the parties in each conflict to secure the support of Rhodes, witness the fact that the island, intrinsically useful because of its geographical position, still wielded considerable power and moral influence.

As early as the 2nd century, and more so in the 1st, Rhodes was an established intellectual and cultural centre. Famous orators like Apollonios Malakos and Apollonios Molon, and philosophers like Poseidonios lived and taught there. These were important personalities for other reasons as well. They were often entrusted with, and carried out successfully, various diplomatic missions, thanks to their connections with the prominent Romans who frequented the island either for political reasons or in search of higher education and cultural contacts. Among such outstanding visitors were persons of no lesser standing than Tiberius Grachus (165 and 161 B.C.), Scipio Emilianus (Africanus the Younger —129 B.C.), Cicero (repeatedly from 78 B.C. onwards), the great poet T. Lucretius Carus (78 B.C.), Julius Caesar (73 and 48 B.C.), Pompey (67 and 63 B.C.), Brutus (58 B.C.), Cato the younger (49 B.C.), Cassius (42 B.C. and earlier for studies), Marcus Antonius (40

B.C.) and many others. In the Late Hellenistic Period, when the great days of Alexandria and Pergamon were at an end, Rhodes was, for the Romans and for any man aspiring to culture, the mainspring of hellenistic thought, literature and art. A few years later, Horace would begin one of his poems with this verse : "Others will praise Rhodes the renowned...,,.

## Roman Period

After his history-making victory at Actium (31 B.C.) at which he defeated Antonius and Cleopatra and remained the sole ruler of the Romans, Octavian (Augustus) gave the Rhodians their "freedom,,, i.e. he granted them local independence in direct dependence on the Roman Emperor instead of assigning them to one of the Roman provinces which were administered and exploited by the Roman generals. But even for this small privilege which allowed them to maintain a measure of economic prosperity for a while longer, the Rhodians were at the mercy of each new emperor, who might, for any reason, leave them, or withdraw from them, their "freedom,,. The strange and perverse Tiberius lived several years (6 B.C. to 2 A.D.) as a semi-exile in Rhodes, as a result of a quarrel with Augustus. He kept so unpleasant a memory of his period of banishment that in later years, he even refused to listen to the Dorian dialect that was still spoken in Rhodes. When he succeeded Augustus on the throne in 14 A.D., the aldermen of Rhodes sent him a letter, the close of which did not include all the usual formal phrases. He summoned them to Rome, made them add the missing phrases, and then let them go. The political exiles of the Roman Period were naturally happy to be allowed to stay in lovely and civilized Rhodes, and Augustus had issued a law allowing them to do so. Nero is reported to have defended the Rhodians, by a speech written in Greek, before Emperor Claudius who had revoked the "freedom,, of Rhodes. Later, too, Nero showed his favour by leaving alone the art treasures of the island, while stripping Olympia, Delphi, and Pergamon of theirs. This alternation of periods of "freedom,, with periods of annexation to the neighbouring Roman provinces lasted for quite a while, until Diocletianus made Rhodes definitely a part of the "Provincia Insularum,, in 297 A.D.

As shown by the Rhodian oration of Dion Chrysostomos (period of Titus), Rhodes still maintained, to some extent, the externals of its greatness, though not its political power, in the 1st century A.D. But in fact Rhodes, like the rest of Greece, was slowly withering away. After the great earthquake of 155 A.D., which "put it upside down,,, Rhodes, for all the financial help provided by Antoninus Pius, never quite recovered. The Rhodian speech of "Ailius Aristeides,, describes its sad decline. True, the Rhodians still held a part of their old dominions on the opposite coast of Asia Minor, and still had their titular rulers (the "prytaneis,,); they still talked of the "freedom and political organisation of the fatherland,,, but hight-sounding words have always been notoriously empty of meaning.

*The town of Rhodes in the early 16th century A.D. (Gabriel).*

In the meantime the Christian religion had begun to strike roots in Rhodes. On his way from Miletus to Syria, Saint Paul stopped at Kos and Rhodes, where numerous Jews were already established in the Hellenistic Period. In the 2nd century, there is in Rhodes a robust Christian community under Bishop Euphranor.

### Middle Ages

A little later, the incursions of the barbarians began from the north. In 263 A.D. the Goths landed on the island and plundered it as they did the Heraion of Samos and the famous Artemission of Ephesos. From now on, and to an even greater extent after the period of the Middle Ages proper (from the 6th century A.D. onwards) the information concerning the historical destinies of the island is fragmentary. This, however, is due rather to the intrinsic character of the events of the medieval —Byzantine or western— history itself. The centre of the state, where history is mainly made, is only loosely connected with the provinces, and the latter retreat, as it were, into the backwaters of history. Historians and chroniclers record only a few striking occurrences —earthquakes, invasions, wars— without any real understanding of internal relationships. There has been no specific neglect of Rhodes

on the part of Byzantium, as has been suggested. Nor does the scarcity of information mean that the Hellenic component of the historic developments of the period was less prominent. Rhodes retained throughout both its Greek character and its own particular features within the Greek world.

In the 7th century A.D. Rhodes was harassed by the Persians under Hosroes, who captured the city during their war with emperor Herakleios (620 A.D.), and later by the Arabs under Moabiah, who sold off the bronze of the famous Colossos that had lain prostrate for centuries (653 A.D.). Then came the frequent invasions by the Saracens, until the Greeks burnt their fleet with the "liquid fire,, in 718. Still later, in the 9th century, the Rhodians were afflicted by the Seltzouks of Aroun al Rashid (807 A.D.). From the 11th century onwards, direct relations with the west are resumed, first in the form of trade with Venice, then through the Crusaders; Rhodian ships take part in the operations; Richard the Lion-Heart of England, and Philip of France arrive with a fleet to recruit mercenaries, in 1191. When the Crusaders captured Constantinople in 1204 A.D. Leon Gavalas, a wealthy land-owner and official of Constantinople declared himself hereditary overlord of Rhodes, and being tolerated by the Venitians, he ruled until 1246, now as an independent ruler, now recognizing the supremacy of the Byzantine emperor. Then the Genoans came, and from 1261 A.D., when the Byzantine emperors recaptured Constantinople, Rhodes was nominally a part of the Byzantine state, but was in fact under the sway of the Genoan admirals of Byzantium.

## Knights and Turks

These various events, associated with the profound decay of Byzantine power, opened the way for the Knights of St. John of Jerusalem. This Order had been created in the 11th century, and its original purposes had been purely religious and charitable. With the permission of the Chalifs of Egypt, the Knights of St. John maintained in Jerusalem a church dedicated to St. John, the patron saint of the Order, as well as a hospital for pilgrims to the Holy Land. In the period of the Crusades, however, the Order participated actively in the wars against the Moslems; so it gradually assumed a military character, and even acquired a castle for its headquarters at Ptolemaïs (Akka, Akra) in the north of Palestine. When the Crusaders finally failed and Ptolemaïs fell in 1291, the Knights of St. John took refuge in Lemessos of Cyprus. In 1306, the Genoan admiral Vignolo, sold them Rhodes, together with Kos and Leros, and by 1309, their establishment in Rhodes was complete.

The Order included three types of members : the Knights (cavallieri), who were in charge of military operations, and whose number never exceeded 500-600; the "brothers„, who were nurses entrusted with the care of the sick; and the clergy who officiated at religious ceremonies. These members who came from all Roman Catholic countries of Europe were further divided into 7 national groups, or "Tongues„, namely those of : Provence, Auvergne, France, Italy, England, Germany and Spain, which was later divided into Aragona and Castiglia. The official languages were Latin and French. The highest administrative authority was the Magister Magnus, elected for life and assisted by a Council, in which the legislative and disciplinary powers were vested.

In the time of the first Great Magister, the autocratic Foulques de Villaret, the Order was torn by internal strife; but the conflicts within the Roman Catholic Church, such as the dissension in the Papal Court of the 14th century and its transfer to Avignon, where some Magisters from Rhodes also came, had immediate repercussions on the Order. On the other hand, trade activity seems to have been considerable during the period of the Knights, in cooperation with the large banking concerns of Western Europe. The Order, further, played an important role in the eastern diplomatic or military affairs of the western European nations in the face of the dangerously increasing Turkish power. Thus the rule of the Knights brought about multiple relations with the West, and these naturally affected the island's culture.

Pressed by the necessity to protect themselves and defend their power against their enemies, the Knights of Rhodes developed a very considerable building activity. The city, probably soon after the great earthquake of 515 A.D., had been greatly reduced in size and had been confined to the area where the castle stands now. The Byzantines had repaired the walls and the moat of the city in 1275. The Knights, however, renovated them according to the requirements of the most advanced military techniques, and built the imposing and very beautiful castle, preserved almost entirely intact to this day. So, with the active help of the inhabitants — for the Knights as we have seen were few in number — and under the very capable leadership of the Great Magister Pierre d'Aubusson, Rhodes was brilliantly successful in resisting the army and fleet sent by Mohamed II the Conqueror to besiege the city in 1480.

However, in 1522, when Villiers de l'Isle-Adam was Great Magister, Sultan Suleiman II, the Magnificent, laid another siege with a very great force. After bravely resisting for 6 months, the Knights lost as a result of treason by one of their own officials and having delivered the city to the Turks on 22nd December 1522, they left for Malta.

Rhodes remained under Turkish rule until 1912. The area within the castle is now inhabited exclusively by Turks. The Turko-Italian war for Tripolis provided the Italians with a pretext for setting foot on the Dodecanese, and they entered Rhodes on 4th May 1912. The sufferings of all the islands of the Dodecanese including Rhodes, under the Italian rule are well-known. The methods already in use for the suppression and uprooting of the Greeks, became more systematic, more complete, more cruel, under the fascist regime. ("Italian Aegean Islands„!). At the end of World War II, the "nymph of the sun„ regained its freedom and was returned to Greece (1945).

# CIVILIZATION AND ART

## The People and its Life

We have seen that in the Homeric Period (8th century B.C.) the "Dorianization,, of Rhodes was already complete. Its civilization however, was not entirely Doric. There are some archaic Rhodian inscriptions written in the Doric dialect but with letters of the Ionian (Miletian) alphabet. This is almost symbolic : the basic framework of the Rhodian civilization was Doric but its external forms were Ionian —in some respects, indeed, more Ionian than any.

The language of Rhodes in late antiquity was a Doric dialect. The common meals prescribed by the Rhodian law for the rulers and "those deciding upon the traditional ways of life,, were very similar to the "pheiditia,, of Sparta. Some of the great public religious festivals of the island were also Doric, as attested by the names of the months in the Rhodian calendar. Such festivals included the "Hyacinthia,,, an ancient Laconic, probably even prehellenic, festival in honour of Apollo and Hyacinth, and the "Karneia,,, a great festival common to all Doric peoples, which was celebrated on the full-moon of the month of September and was dedicated to Apollo Karneios , patron god of flocks. Herakles, the father of their progenitor Tlepolemos, was also worshipped. The "Sminthia,,, a festival dedicated to Dionysos Sminthios, included theatrical performances. But even the names of some months already show traces of the Ionian influence, especially the month "Dalios,, so named after the Delian Apollo, and reflecting the great importance of the Delian Amphictyonia in the Archaic Period. Other important cults, such as the cult of the Lindian Athene, seem to be combinations of Greek with local, i.e. prehellenic, religious traditions.

Gradually, the H a l i e i a, the festival of the Sun, came to be the most important festival. This ancient God is distinct from Apollo, though the latter absorbed in many places part of the worship of the former; both the form and the myths connected with the Sun-god are more directly and more sensually related to the natural phenomenon. The Sun-god was also worshipped in many other Doric places, e.g. in Lakonia, Arcadia, Elis, Corinthia (Akrokorinthos), A r g o l i s. It would appear that the Doric immigrants brought this cult with them from their original home place and, coming to Rhodes found there some similar prehellenic cult which they assimilated to their own. So the Sun became a very important element in the religion of the Rhodians, a fact reflected also in the particular myths of Rhodes (the most

important of which are included in Pindar's hymn). The cult of the Sun was probably common to all three cities of Rhodes even prior to the Synoecism and as holy rites do not change easily, it can be assumed that the centre of worship was situated in the area where the new city was built in 408 B.C. After the Synoecism, however, it became the central, official religion of the new political organization. The "S m a l l  H a l i e i a,, were celebrated each year in the month Panamos (July-August). A more important festival was the "G r e a t  H a l i e i a,,, celebrated every four years in the leap month Panamos b (d i p a n a m i a  H a l i e i a). The festivities included gymnic games, musical contests (guitar, etc.), and chariot races; official delegations (theoriai) of other cities often attended. The Rhodians had a strange custom, reported by a Roman author : each year they dedicated a chariot to the Sun and threw it into the sea, because they believed that the sun used such a vehicle to circle the earth.

From existing ancient sources of information and from their history and civilization, it would appear that the Rhodians were a nation of down-to-earth realists; without too much imagination or spontaneity, they were careful in their calculations, with a tendency to conservatism but capable of adjusting to change, endowed with an equal measure of sentiment and rationality; their way of life was simple, denoting a love of order and a repulsion to any lack of balance or measure. It is reported for example that anyone disembarking at the port of Rhodes in the 1st century B.C. realized immediately, from the manners of the people that this was no Syrian or Cilician town, but an ancient Greek city; there were no people running hastily in the streets, and in the theatre they watched quietly, indicating their approval by a slight smacking of the lips. They were very careful not to break any religious rules. A pertinent example : when Artemisia, the widow of Mausolus, defeated the Rhodians in 351 B.C. she set up a bronze trophy, consisting of two statues, representing Artemisia stigmatizing the personified city of Rhodes. Every trophy, however, was sacred to the gods, and so the Rhodians, having regained their freedom but not daring to offend the gods, had a high wall built around that humiliating symbol and declared the place taboo (abaton). Also, during the famous siege by Demetrios, they respected his father's, Antigonos, and his own statues, for even statues set up in honour of humans were still in some way dedicated to the gods, and therefore the Rhodians left them intact, though some proposed to the "Ecclesia„ that they be destroyed; it has, however, been suggested, at least by Diodorus, that this was an act of political expediency rather than of religious reverence, comparable to their decision not to injure Mithridates' statue, while the latter was besieging their city at a later date.

There are several ancient jokes, making fun of the Rhodian habit to split hairs about trifles. As one story (Rhodion chresmos) has it, the Rhodians used to sacrifice every day to the Lindian Athene, whereupon they would sit in the sanctuary and feast on the sacrificial meats; it had not been their habit, however, to bring any chamber pots with them and one day they set about wondering whether perhaps they might. They sent somebody to ask Apollo, and the god gave permission. But then the question arose whether the chamber pots should be clay or bronze. Being unable to decide the issue, they sent to Apollo again, but the god had had enough and returned the oracle: "neither!„ More often the Rhodians are described as people who liked fun and appreciated the good things of life; and, naturally, life in this port city which was "hardly less sophisticated than Athens„ would not be exactly gloomy. There was no lack of good eating (witness Athenaeus "D e i p n o s o p h i s t a i„) and drinking, gambling, and gay and eager "she-friends„. Their mildness and humaness are also exalted : the executioner was forbidden entry into city; in the beginning of Demetrios' siege, they reached an agreement with the enemy, that prisoners of war on either side would not be killed or sold as slaves, but would be returned against a ransom fixed in advance at 1000 drachmas for freemen, and 500 drachmas for slaves.

But above all, the Rhodians were known as seamen and merchants. There was a saying : "ten Rhodians, ten ships„. The ancient authors speak with admiration of the experience and skill of Rhodian skippers. Polybios mentions that there was a Carthaginian who was so excellent a ship's captain, his friends had nicknamed him "Rhodian„. They were celebrated for their craftsmanship as ship-builders; they had devised new types of sea-craft for trade and transportation, for chasing sea-robbers (the fast, public "phylakides„), for their war fleet which protected the city, and for their commercial fleet, which was not always very large, but was manned with outstanding crews. Cicero, however, who was no sailor, having travelled in the period of the summer-winds in July from Piraeus to Delos on a Rhodian "open„ craft (a ship covered fore and aft but open to the sky in the middle) complained that though it was quick, it rocked terribly. The many ship-shaped monuments of Lindos show how much the Rhodians enjoyed a well-designed vessel even in the artistic sense.

In terms of their sea-trade, they had enacted, at an early date, civilized laws ensuring the protection of the traders' interests and encouraging foreigners to entrust their merchandise to Rhodian cargo - vessels. This set of laws, which constitute the very first marine code in the world, was praised highly by Cicero, was introduced by Augustus to the whole Roman empire, and a century and a half later, Antoninus Pius ordered every difficult seatrade problem resolved according to the old Rhodian laws.

Parts of these laws found their way into "Vassilika„ by Leon the Wise and into the "Hexabiblos„ of Armenopoulos - ("the marine code of the Rhodians„) but it is impossible to tell whether these extracts are genuinely ancient. A provision relating to "general average„

*Portrait-head of the comic poet Menandros (Rhodes museum).*

*Poseidonios from Apameia*
*Portrait-head of the philosopher*
*(Naples, National museum).*

*Relief from the tomb of Hieronymos (Berlin, Hiller von Gaertringen Collection).*

(lex Rhodia de iactu), adapted by Augustus, is characteristic : if throwing some merchandise into the sea resulted in saving the rest of the cargo, then the party whose goods had been lost, was entitled to compensation from the others. They also had laws relating to the rules to be observed in the use of ports. For instance, if a ship having too long an iron boom entered the port, it was confiscated.

## Culture

The mental agility and the openness of mind with which sea-trade has traditionally endowed the Mediterranean peoples, when coupled with the right temperament, is conducive to the development of culture, and Rhodes did become an important cultural centre. Several poets, writers, and artists were born there as elsewhere, but the main feature in Rhodes consisted in the creation of a climate which favoured the development and preservation of culture, of a long, uninterrupted tradition that means the population's need for culture. Cicero later referred to the Rhodians as "highly educated,, people. This attracted many foreign thinkers and artists who, by establishing themselves and working there contributed as much as their local counterparts to the particular culture of Rhodes. Few regions in Ionia or, for that matter, in Greece proper —with the exception of incomparable Athens— developed an individual culture of any duration. Rhodes stood above them all.

It was only after the Rhodian state had assumed its final form as an autonomous organization with its own economic and political aims, that the island became a centre of intellectual and educational activity, though it had been a centre of art before that. Individual men of letters, especially poets, however, had appeared very early. In the late 7th century B.C. P e i-s a n d r o s, son of Peison from Kamiros, related the story of Herakles, the mythical ancestor of the Rhodians, in the epic poem "Herakleia,,; he was the first to describe Herakles with the lion-hide and the club, which from then on became the typical symbols of Herakles in Greek art; for the ancients appreciated Peisandros very highly, considering him second only to Homer and Hesiodos. The city of Rhodes, in the 3rd century B.C., honoured his memory with a bronze statue, the inscription to which was provided by Theocritos.

In the first half of the 6th century, an important personality in the intellectual world, comparable to Solon of Athens, was K l e o b o u l o s, son of Evagoras from Lindos, who, as we have seen earlier, was in addition a politician of note. He was considered one of the seven wise men of antiquity, and he was the author of the famous dictum "measure is best,,. He played a part in the modification of the sanctuary of the Lindian Athene, and he was reputed as the author of the "swallow-song,, which the children sang from door to door collecting money for the temple. To him was further attributed a fine tomb inscription for one Midas, characterized by a fresh and expansive sense of nature in the Ionian style — later criticized by Simonides as being improper in its meaning.

During the Persian Wars, T i m o k r e o n of Ialyssos wrote "Songs,,, some verses of which have been preserved. The ancients described Timokreon as vainglorious, a glutton, and a malicious gossip. A former friend of Themistokles, he quarrelled with him when Themistokles failed to ensure his return to his home city of Ialyssos from which he had been banished on a charge of collaboration with the Persians — and accused Themistokles and the latter's friend Simonides with some viciously virulent verses. Simonides retaliated later with his well-known epigram.

In the first half of the 4th century, A n a x a n d r i d e s of Kamiros acquired fame as a writer of comedies and dithyrambs. He wrote 65 comedies and was a victor at the "Lenaia„ games of Athens in the year 377 B.C. and on two other occasions later.

It is at this time approximately that Rhodes begins to attract foreign intellectuals. The Cyrenaean A r i s t i p p o s, a disciple of Socrates, becomes a teacher in the gymnasium of Rhodes. When the famous Athenaean orator A e s c h i n e s, in 330 B.C. lost a case to Ktesiphon and Demosthenes (it was on this occasion that the latter pronounced his famous oration "on the crown„), he left Athens in disgust and settled down in Rhodes and its vicinity, where he taught the art of public speaking. Some letters from these parts have come down to us. Their genuineness is disputed by some, but it is a fact that they show a good knowledge of the area. Aeschines was considered the founder of the Rhodian school of rhetoric, but no famous orators from this school are known until the 2nd century B.C.

The peripatetic philosophy is introduced to Rhodes in the late 4th century by the Rhodian E u d e m o s, one of the best pupils of Aristotle and the master's favourite. He remained faithful to his teacher's system and worked hard on an edition of Aristotle's writings, e.g. "Metaphysika„, though he left it unfinished at his death. He also wrote some works of his own, and Aristotle's "Ethika Eudemeia„ has been attributed to him. Other peripatetic philosophers in Rhodes were P r a x i p h a n e s and I e r o n y m o s in the following century.

A well-known writer and poet of the early 3rd century is S i m i a s the Rhodian. He wrote "various poems„, lyrics, epigrams and the so-called "technopaignia„; these were poems consisting of verses of varying length which, written one beneath the other, formed various shapes such as eggs, axes, wings. Some of these poems have been preserved, and they are amusing.

But a much more important poet of this period is A p o l l o n i o s the Rhodian (ca. 295-215 B.C.), so called, although he was born in Alexandria or Naukratis, because he spent most of his life, and died, in Rhodes where he taught philology and was made a citizen "honoris causa„. While in Alexandria, he had studied under the poet Kallimachos, later becoming director of the famous library. He left Alexandria as a result of a violent quarrel with his master about the art of poetry. From the many poems he wrote (including one entitled; "The creation of Rhodes„), only "Argonautika„ has been preserved. This is a short epos, typical of the new poesy of the Hellenistic Period, passionate, and written in a flowery and involved style. Apart from its interest in terms of the historical development of literature, the poem has true poetic value. It was highly appreciated and widely imitated by the ancients, including Virgil.

In the second half of the 3rd century, the Rhodian K a l l i x e n o s, a writer and, perhaps, also a sculptor wrote an "Enumeration of painters and statue-makers,,, and a book "on Alexandria,,. Athenaeus preserved a large part of the latter, including a description of a famous procession organized by Ptolemy II (Philadelphos) in 274 B.C., and of the "exceedingly magnificent stage,, set up by the Court artists for the banquet. This detailed description, a very valuable source of information about hellenistic architecture, proves Kallixenos an expert in artistic matters.

Science in general was also cultivated in Rhodes. From the fact that many ancient investigators assumed the Equator (from the Herculaean Pillars to India) and the principal meridian (from Maroc in Egypt to Byzantium) to cross at Rhodes; that Atabyrion was one of the first mountains whose height was measured; that long geographical distances are often calculated with reference to Rhodes; that several astronomical observations, e.g. that the longest day is 14-and-a-half hours long, are associated with Rhodes; it would appear that Rhodes was one of the main centres for the study of astronomy and geography. The eminent astronomer and mathematician H i p p a r c h o s from Nicaia (in Bithynia) made his first astronomical observation in Rhodes in the year 161 B.C., lived on the island for many years thereafter, and his work was taken up by others after him.

Philological studies were also flourishing. The renowned Dionysios from Thrace (170-90 B.C.), a disciple of the great Aristarchos, and writer of many philological texts including the very important "on grammar,, which was the principal textbook on grammar down to the Renaissance, lived and taught, for the most part, in Rhodes. Timachidas of Lindos, son of Agesitimos, also a philologist and a historian, is of interest mainly as the author of the famous large inscription of Lindos (now in Copenhagen), known as the "Chronicle of the Temple of Lindos,, and dating from 99 B.C., which is a listing of the most precious votive offerings to Athene—both mythical and real—made to the temple, and of the greatest miracles performed by the goddess "epifaneia,, (revealings). The inscription is 2.37 m. high and 0,85 m. wide.

The widespread reputation of Rhodes as the most important centre of culture and learning in the late Hellenistic Period, was mainly due to its philosophers and orators. The stoic philosopher Panaetios, son of Nicagoras (185-110 B.C.), a descendant of a noble Rhodian family, was one of Rhodes' most brilliant sons. His ancestors, so Strabo tells us and Lindian inscriptions confirm, were "army leaders and memorable athletes,,. A widely travelled cosmopolitan, Panaetios spent most of his life abroad. He had many influential friends in Rome —and these were useful for Rhodes— and he was a close friend of Scipio Africanus the Younger, whom he accompanied on many a diplomatic mission and military expedition. Later, he went to Athens, where he became head of the stoic school. His philosophical theory is dominated by the ethical and the rational, and represents a mitigation of the sharp contrasts between the other philosophical systems (Platonic, Aristotelian); his best-known work is a treatise "on duty,,.

The mystical element was more prominent in his important pupil, the famous P o s e i d o n i o s (135 - 51 B.C.). Born at Apameia of Syria and widely travelled himself, he first succeeded his teacher as head of the school of Athens in 110 B.C., then travelled for many years to various parts of the world, and finally settled in Rhodes in 90 B.C. and stayed there until his death. The Rhodians held him in great esteem. They elected him twice to the highest office (one of the 5 prytaneis), entrusted him with important missions in Rome (to Marius, Sulla, and others). Prominent Romans like Pompey, Cicero, a.o. would come to Rhodes to be his pupils, and then his friends. He was altogether an outstanding personality, and had indeed been referred to as the "last great mind of antiquity,,. He wrote several historical works with special reference to the cultures and customs of various peoples, as well as geographical, cosmological, mathematical and, naturally, philosophical treatises, including one in which he expounded a theory "on soothsaying and demons,,. His influence upon later generations of thinkers was immeasurable, but of his many writings only a few fragments have been preserved. Finally, the Rhodian peripatetic philosopher A n d r o n i k o s deserves our gratitude for it was he who, in 60-50 B.C., first and very carefully, published the writings of Aristotle known as "internal,,, i.e. intended exclusively for his own disciples, which had been lost until then.

No less renowned were the orators of Rhodes in this period. In 121 B.C., the great orator A p o l l o n i o s  M a l a k o s from Alabanda of Asia Minor settled in Rhodes, followed shortly by his compatriot A p o l- l o n i o s  M o l o n, a contemporary of Poseidonios. This Apollonios acquired great fame and Romans of the highest standing such as Cicero and Julius Caesar, were among his students. He also carried out important diplomatic missions on behalf of the Rhodians. With its teaching of rhetoric, both theoretical and practical, the school of Rhodes, a continuation of the school of Asia Minor, the so-called "Asianism,,, represents the transition to the "Atticism,, of the years of Augustus. "Asianism,, with its pomposity, its love of simile and exaggeration, its involved structure, and its passion, was a typical manifestation of the hellenistic spirit. The Rhodian school tempered these characteristics with a measure of classicism, a return to Attic models, and simplicity. But as the roots of the Rhodian tradition were hellenistic, Molon, characteristically preferred the elegant and brilliant Hyperides to the more sober Demosthenes. In the midst of so pervading a rhetoric activity, it was almost unavoidable that an enemy would appear : the Rhodian A t h e n o d o r o s wrote a book purporting to prove that rhetoric was not an art.

In a place where learning was so highly appreciated, there certainly existed schools and libraries. Little is known about their organization, but some pieces of accidental information are characteristic. When e.g. the king of Pergamon Eumenes presented the Rhodians in 160 B.C. with 200,000 medimnoi of wheat to sell and use the interest of the proceeds "to pay salaries to the instructors and teachers of their sons,,, he must have known that such a gift would please them. A tomb inscription from the end of the 3rd century, honours the memory of a teacher who, having taught school for 52 years, went to the "area of the pious,,; the interesting r e l i e f probably belonging to the same tomb, the work of a sculptor named D e m e t r i o s, shows this teacher first among his pupils and then among the gods of the other world; the teacher was one Ieronymos, son of Simylinos, a Tloan, and he may have been the same as the peripatetic philosopher of that name. Another tomb inscription praises the virtues of the "ever memorable,, Arideikes "whom the Muses reared

with motherly hands on the platonic ways,,; so this must be the famous platonic philosopher Arideikes, a pupil of the great Arkesilaos, and ambassador of the Rhodians during their war with Byzantium in 220 B.C. Collections of books, both private and public
were necessary for teaching, and for the philological and other scientific studies pursued at
Rhodes. In the early part of the 3rd century, Ptolemy Philadelphos, got some books from
Rhodes for the library of Alexandria. An insciption dating from the 2nd century B.C.
includes parts of the list of books belonging to one gymnasium of Rhodes, with names of
various works, number of copies and names of donors.

## Art

*«τηλόθεν ἐκ νήσοιο Ρόδου τέχνασμα ποθεινὸν»*
*(ἐπίγραμμα Βηρυτοῦ)*

An amazing number of large and small works of art have been found
in Rhodes but only a few of these remain on the island. The study of this
valuable material, both published and unpublished, is not yet as advanced
as it could and should have been. Many points relating to the sequence of
artistic events and to the particular physiognomy of Rhodian artistic creation still remain obscure. What we do know with certainty is that the Rhodian
artistic production was highly appreciated in other countries, and very much
in demand from an early age. It also had considerable influence on the art
of the places to which it was exported. Rhodes had developed a distinct
artistic tradition, which workshops all over the world were trying to emulate
or imitate. After the "Synoecism,,, and for many centuries to come, Rhodes
became a true home of the arts, always in search of novel aesthetic emotions,
a pole of attraction for foreign artists from all over, a place where local and
foreign traditions cross, breed and merge, creating important new currents
—though these have not yet been clearly untangled at present.

Works of M y c e n a e a n art, i.e. pottery and jewellery dating from the
period of the pre-Dorian Greeks, the Achaeans, have been found in great
profusion, especially in the tombs of Kamiros and Ialyssos.

This type of art, an offshoot of the Minoan, is indifferent to architectural consequence in either the form or the decoration of pots, getting its
inspiration mostly from the vegetal, and the marine animal world. Such works
were manufactured on the island but were also imported.

In the period between 1100 and 1000 B.C., a new style is developed,
the so-called g e o m e t r i c, a pure hellenic style, whose most classical
creations were produced in Attica around 850-750 B.C. Now the spirit of
strict architectural form reigns supreme, in the form of the pot itself as
well as in the arrangement and the combination of decorations. The new
style abhors the elusive polymorphy of the organic world, and uses exclusively pure geometric forms (circles, triangles, maeanders, etc.) or, if it
does use organic shapes (men, animals, plants) it transforms them into
geometric forms. In Rhodes,which is now decidedly Doric, as in the rest of
the Greek world, the new style quickly becomes dominant, but here, in the
vicinity of the oriental, Ionian, sphere of influence, it assumes a more co-
lorful aspect, its forms are softer and have the beauty of a carpet (pl. 4).

Around 700 B.C., Greek art is fertilized by yet another current : the
so-called "oriental,, period leads to a marked relaxation of the severity of

geometric forms; those are not eliminated, but they are enriched with profuse, luxuriant decorative elements representing both real and imaginary beings, a wealth of themes from natural vegetation that seems almost to be spilling out of the decorated sufrace. In the lovely Rhodian pottery of the period, the dense decorative designs, painted upon a white coat, finely drawn but lacking the hard lines of the workshops of the mainland, convey mainly an effect of colour (pl. 2).

A reversal of trend occurs at about 650 B.C. Greek art makes an impression as if it stopped for a moment to gather its forces, and then, guided by its inherent geometric tendency, it set about rearranging in a more orderly and disciplined fashion the achievements of orientalism. This is the "d a e - d a l i c,, period, associated with the famous, almost legendary figure of the sculptor Daedalos. It is now that Greek art, enriched by the plentiful organic material infused into it by "orientalism,,, creates with the certainty ensured to it by the solid base of the geometric rules, the first really great plastic as well as architectural monuments. All Greek countries are more or less involved in this universal change of heart and mind; but the purest and most original and lasting masterpieces came out of the Doric workshops of Crete and the Peloponnese.

Rhodes, a Doric offshoot transplanted in an Ionian environment, reacted in her own particularly attractive way and became a significant factor in the new movement. Pindar, in his ode to Diagoras (written in 464 B.C.), provided the earliest testimony concerning the excellence and fame of the artists of archaic Rhodes "...the grey-eyed goddess herself bestowed upon them every art, so that they surpassed all mortal men by their deftness of hand and along the roads rose works of art l i k e u n t o b e i n g s t h a t l i v e d a n d m o v e d; and great was their fame. Yet, to the wise man, even surpassing art is no magic power,,. With these words, Pindar attributes to the Rhodian artists the very virtues of Daedalos as described in the ancient myths — a fact confirmed by the ancient Commentators. The art that is "free of fraud,, is a reference to the "fraudulent,, art of the prehellenic Telchines.

*Rhodian vases dating from the 7th c. B.C. (Rhodes museum)*

At a later date (3rd century B.C.), the poet Kallimachòs recorded the fact that in Samos, the first idol of Hera was a shapeless plank, very similar to that of the Lindian Athene. The new statue was made by one Skelmis; other sources refer to this artist as Smilis from Aegina. The two names are synonymous and so are the corresponding generic terms "smile,, and "skalme,, ( = a chisel or a "Thracian knife,, as the ancients called it). Skelmis, on the other hand, was the name of one of the Telchines —so, in a round about way we are back to Rhodes again. Finally, a statue of the Lindian Athene, which was burnt in Constantinople in 476 A.D., was reputed to be a work of Dipaenos and Skyllis, disciples of Daedalos, who had worked in several parts of Greece around 600 B.C. This statue was looking like Egyptian and it was made of a strange material, "emerald or some other stuff,, according to the Byzantines. This is reminiscent of the cauldron dedicated by the Telchines to Athene, which, according to the Chronicle of Lindos, no one could tell what it was made of. So, written evidence seems to point to Rhodes as a daedalic centre. As to the mingling of historical fact and mythical remembrance, we have pointed out earlier that to the mind of the early Greeks, history and myth are one. Skelmis, a mixture of fact and fancy, may well have been the Rhodian counterpart of Daedalos, himself a half-historical, half-mythical figure.

It is true that there are in Rhodes no plastic monuments of that period which might shed light on the testimony of the ancients. But the gaps of our knowledge are still very great. Some years ago, nothing was known about the daedalic works of Crete. Moreover, as Rhodes has no marble suitable for statues, the Rhodian craftsmen worked with metal to a far greater extent. The very legends about the Telchines suggest an extensive use of metal. The earliest large plastic monuments would have been made of hammered iron around a wooden core. But such statues are seldom preserved. On the other hand, many smaller samples of Rhodian metal-craft have come down to us, such as the fine gold jewels found at several places but especially in the tombs of Kamiros, some of them indeed together with Psammitichus' scarabee; they consist of small gold plates decorated with a combination of wirework, granulation and relief forming various ornamental designs and figures of goddesses, sphinxes, centaurs, etc. These jewels show an excellent craftsmanship as well as aesthetic sense and reflect strongly the daedalic spirit combined with an oriental influence that makes them more "juicy,, than the products of the western workshops. The diadem in this page is a representative example.

*Golden jewellery representing a winged Artemis dating from the 7th c. B.C. (British museum).*

The same marked daedalic spirit can be seen in pottery-painting —both in the overal composition and in the particular elements going into it. A typical example is the well-known plate representing Menelaos and Hector fighting around the body of Euforbos, from the last decade of the 7th century. Narrative paintings are rare. The large closed jars are decorated with successive stripes of many wild animal figures; in the smaller, open and shallow bowls, decorative flower and plant designs on the white coat are exquisitely balanced on the curved surfaces.

Rhodian pottery painters continue to produce fine work in the next century; the pots of Fikellura (so named after the place where they were first found) were exported on a large scale. A specimen can be seen in plate 3, 6-9. In the 5th century, when the technically and artistically incomparable products of Attica had reduced all other workshops including those of Rhodes, to insignificance, Rhodes continued to produce simple pottery for everyday uses. A Rhodian potter proudly notes on a small amphora that the best pottery clay can be found in Brassia, in Western Rhodes.

Some samples of archaic stoneware pottery have also been found in Rhodes. Apart from the statuettes of porous stone which were inexpensive offerings to the gods like those made of clay elsewhere, and being perfunctorily worked, provide little information on Rhodian artistic culture, a few marble heads and bodies of kouroi were found in Kamiros (pl. 10, 11). Some of these were made in other island workshops. But if a head found in Constantinople and dating from 540 B.C. approximately, is indeed — as it is supposed to be — a Rhodian work, which combines the excellent quality of the sculpture with the softness of the painting, then the high artistic level of the island is very clean.

A high artistic level is also attested to by Rhodian pottery from the early 7th century well into the 5th century; of this, we have a large number of specimens, because their use was widespread in many parts of the ancient world; they include plastic pots (pl.14)i.e. pots shaped in the form of human bodies or heads, animal figures, clay figurines intended for use as offerings to temples or tombs like the finely chiselled head of a goddess shown in plate 12, which was found in a tomb in Kamiros; it dates from around 500 B.C. and even its colours have been well preserved. The exquisite 5th century relief of Crito and Timarista shown in plate 17, bearing the unmistakable signs of Ionian influence, would be inconceivable if the good tradition had been entirely cut off. While it is difficult to define exactly its particular characteristics, it is obvious that Rhodian artistic production in all branches of the arts has always been significant, at times even exemplary, and that these Dorian islanders were not isolated in, but fruitfully fertilized by, their Ionian environment.

Like intellectual activity, the artistic life underwent a radical change with the "Synoecism,, of 408 B.C., as a result of which Rhodes became a factor of universal rather than local or provincial historical significance. For many centuries thereafter, there is a dazzling variegated multitude of artistic names, works and trends. When the Rhodians now invite celebrated foreign artists to work on the island, or when they buy their works, these acts carry quite a different weight as compared to the Archaic Period. The limited parochial outlook of the local workshop is gradually replaced by each individual artist's increased awareness of his personality, his purposes, and his methods.

Not long after this change was initiated, the great classical painter P a r- r a s i o s appears on the scene. Parrasios was the son of Euenor of Ephe- sos, a painter and sculptor who worked mainly in Athens in the late 5th and early 4th century. The ancients admired in particular Parrasios' design, and the way he was able to suggest depth and volume by the clever shaping of contours. One of his paintings, representing the three heroes Meleagros, Herakles and Perseus, was in Rhodes. More of his works were kept at Lindos : one represented Herakles, presumably in some unusual form, because the painter had thought it necessary to add an inscription explaining that he often dreamt of Herakles in that form. A little later, towards the middle of the 4th century, the important sculptor of Attica, Bryaxis, who had worked with Skopas, Timotheos and Leochares, on the sculptures for the Mausoleum of Alikarnassos, was commissioned to provide 5 colossal statues of gods for Rhodes.

Interestingly, the most important artists who worked in the immediate environment of Alexander the Great were associated with Rhodes. The great L y s i p p o s —known as the father of hellenistic art in the sense that Michelangelo has been called the father of baroque— and Alexander's favourite portrait-maker, had made the famous bronze quadriga with Helios on it for Rhodes. This was also a work of colossal dimensions, since Cassius left it in Rhodes because he was unable to transport it. The gold chariot of Helios dedicated at approximately the same time by the city of Rhodes to Apollo in Delphi and whose pedestal was found behind the tripod of Plataiae, must have been similar. Another statue by Lysippos was at Lindos, the base of which, bearing the signature of the artist, has been found. Of the great painter A p e l l e s, another favourite of Alexander's, there were two portraits in Rhodes, showing the king of Caria Menandros and one Angaeos or Antaeos, both apparently "associates,, of Alexander's. Apelles, however, is associated with Rhodes mainly through his connection with the great Rhodian painter Protogenes.

The most famous of Alexander's architects, D e i n o c r a t e s, was something more —he was, according to the most reliable sources, a Rhodian himself. It was him the great king appointed to lay out the plan of Alexandria. He was responsible for the magnificent "pyre,, of Hephaistion, in Babylon, ordered by Alexander the Great when he decided to honour his beloved friend by a burial of unprecedented pomp and splendour. The "pyre,, was a gigantic tomb consisting of several stories and decorated with all kinds of precious statues. But the most ambitious plan conceived by Deinocrates and suggested by him to Alexander, involved the transformation of the whole of Mt. Athos into one enormous statue of Alexander.

With its feet, the statue would touch the sea, and with its left arm it would embrace a town where 10.000 inhabitants would live; its left hand would hold a huge bowl into which would flow all the waters of the mountain, from there to pour in a cascade down to the sea like a libation. This he told Alexander, would be "the most permanent and most prominent,, of his statues, "as it would have eternal roots in i n d e s t r u c t i b l e  a n d l i v i n g  m a t t e r, and its weight would make it immovable and immutable...,,, whereas his other statues were the works of "cowardly and ignoble craftsmen,,. Alexander, however, refused for he remembered what had happened to Xerxes and feared the wrath of the gods. But though this sweeping project never came to anything, its very conception, characterized, as Plutarch put it, by "love of greatness, boldness and arrogance,,, has the flavour of the spirit of the Hellenistic Period. It is interesting that the artists of a corresponding period of later era,the exponents of baroque, were fascinated by Deinokrates' idea and some of them, e.g. the Italian painter Pietro da Cortona (1596 - 1669) and the historically more interesting great Austrian architect J.B. Fischer von Erlach (1656 - 1723), actually attempted to work out its form and manner of execution.

Rhodes probably made another contribution to hellenistic architecture, as can be inferred from the fact that a particular kind of colonnade (an inner courtyard surrounded by columns) where the arcade looking to the south is higher than the other three, was called "Rhodian,,. Examples of this type of colonnade can be seen in Delos, e.g. in the "house of the masks,,.

The most famous artist of Rhodes in the late 4th century was the painter P r o t o g e n e s, a native of Caunos in Caria, who spent most of his life and did most of his work in Rhodes. He was also a sculptor in bronze and, in addition, author of a theoretical book "on graphic and shapes,,. His great colleague and contemporary, Apelles, admired him greatly. He used to buy his works and on one occasion he wrote that he was left speechless by one of his paintings —Ialyssos. He recognized in him an artist of equal if not higher value than himself, and would find in him only one shortcoming: that he was unable to take his hand off the painting in time and that by working over and over at the details, he destroyed the grace and lightness that made his own —Apelles'— creations "touch the heavens,,. It is indeed on record that Protogenes would retouch his paintings over and again in successive layers for years before he was satisfied, all the while eating very little to prevent dulling of his senses. He was not a profuse producer. Two or three of his paintings were sent to Athens and there were a few portraits including one of king Antigonos (father of the Poliorcet) and one of Artistotle's mother. Aristotle had tried in vain to persuade him to paint the deeds of Alexander.

His best-known work was the "Dionysion,, of Rhodes : a series of paintings representing the personages of the mythical history of the island, and more particularly Ialyssos, the hero after whom the city of Ialyssos was named. In the painting, Ialyssos was represented as a hunter accompanied by his panting dog. Protogenes is said to have worked on it for 7 or 11 years. Another famous painting was the so-called "Resting Satyr,,; holding his flutes, he was leaning against a column, and on top of this stood a partridge. Both of these works are associated with the famous siege by Demetrios. The legends said that Demetrios missed several opportunities to take the city, just because he would not risk destroying these masterpieces with fire. The painter's workshop, we are told, was in a garden outside the walls of the city, and when Demetrios asked him if he was not afraid, the painter replied that he was not, for, he said : "I know that thou art at war with the Rhodians but not with the arts,,.

The celebrated C o l o s s o s was also connected with Demetrios' siege; Proud of their victory, the Rhodians used the proceeds of the sale of Demetrios' siege machines (300 talanta) to errect a triumphant statue of their God Helios. C h a r e s of Lindos, a pupil of Lysippos, was commissioned to execute the project, and it took him twelve years (from 304 to 292 B.C. approximately) to complete it. He cast the various parts of the statue one by one, into huge heaps of earth on the spot, proceeding from the feet upwards in successive stages as one would build a house with several floors. Its height was 70 ells ( = approx. 31 metres), but that is about all we know about it, except the head, of which we got an idea from contemporary and later Rhodian coins. The statue was praised by Lucianos "for the craftsmanship and accuracy of the execution with so large a size,,, and the ancients in general counted this outstanding technical and artistic achievement among the seven wonders of the world. The "wonder,,, however, did not stand upright for more than 66 years : at the great earthquake of 226 B.C., it broke at the knees and "shook many houses in its fall,,. Having been frightened by some oracle, the Rhodians did not attempt to restore it.

So the Colossos lay prostrate for many centuries causing those who looked at it from close by to wonder at its internal construction; in the deep caves that gaped from its broken limbs, you could see the iron riggings and the heavy blocks of rock Chares had used to ensure the solidity and the stability of the Colossos; few men could embrace its thumb; its fingers were bigger than many a whole statue. Finally, in 653 A.D., when the Arabs under Moabiah plundered Rhodes, they hauled the fragments of the Colossos to the coast across the sea and sold it as bronze to a Jew from Edessa; the buyer had to use 900 camels to transport it. The legend of the Colossos, however, remained so closely associated with Rhodes, that in the medieval period, the Rhodians were referred to as "Colossians,, by both Greeks and Latins. Younger generations have tried to imagine where the Colossos might have stood, and for centuries now the myth has been accepted that it straddled the entrance of the port so that the ships passed between its legs, and that it held in its hand a light that shone over a great distance. This erroneous belief arose probably from a misunderstanding of the ancient inscription on the base of the statue, which read as follows :

> To thy very self, O Sun, did the people of Dorian Rhodes raise high to heaven this colossos,[1] then, when having laid to rest the brazen wave of war, they crowned their country with the spoils of their foes. Not only over the sea, but on the land, too, did they establish the lovely light of unfettered freedom. For to those who spring from the race of Heracles dominion is a heritage both on land and sea.
>
> 1. Chares of Lindus made the Colossos of Rhodes, eighty cubits high.

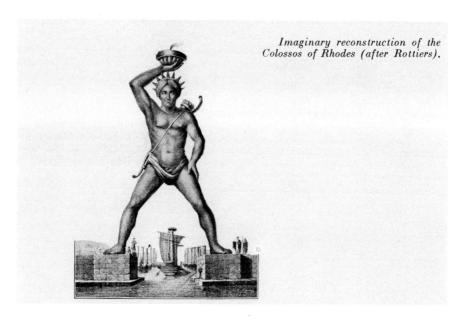

Imaginary reconstruction of the Colossos of Rhodes (after Rottiers).

One thing is certain : that it stood on land. Were it otherwise, the ancients would certainly not have failed to comment on the fact; besides, its construction, from what we know about it, would certainly require a foundation on solid land; and finally, had it stood over the entrance of the port, it would have tumbled into the sea, when it fell during the earthquake. The exact location however, remains unknown, though it must have been in the vicinity of the ports. The pier of St. Nicholas has been suggested, but seems improbable. A more likely hypothesis points to the area of St. John's church of the Knights, which no longer exists but was known in the Middle Ages as St. Johannes Colossensis.

Another colossal head by the same sculptor Chares existed in Rome at a later date. It seems that the Rhodians had a liking for such outsized ornaments in their city. We have already referred to the five colossal works of Bryaxis and to Lysippos' quadriga. Pliny mentions that there were a hundred colossi of a smaller size than the Colossos of Chares in Rhodes each one of which would suffice to make any place famous.

These facts constitute in themselves unmistakable signs of the new age that had begun with the successors of Alexander —the Hellenistic Period. And it is an indisputable fact that the art of Rhodes forms an important aspect of h e l l e n i s t i c art. Testimonies, both written and monumental (and to the latter should be counted perhaps the monuments of the neighbouring islands, e.g. the plentiful material of Kos) there are many, but most of the information is still unprocessed, unconfirmed and with many gaps. Nevertheless, evidence of the significance of Rhodes during this period does crop up again and again. The beautiful head of a fighting Gaul now kept at the Cairo museum, for instance, was most probably found in Rhodes, and it is a very important work dating from about 200 B.C., halfway through the Hellenistic Period.

*Bronze statue of Eros (N. York, Metropolitan museum).*

It was in Rhodes too in all likelihood, that another valuable monument of approximately the same period was found : the bronze statue —lately acquired by the museum of New York— of a life-size sleeping Eros sprawled upon a rock. It is strongly reminiscent of the child holding, and nearly choking, a goose, a famous work of Boethos' of Chalcedon; there may in fact exist a deeper relation between the two works than a mere external similarity.

B o e t h o s from Chalcedon of Bithynia, a well-known bronze craftsman and engraver, who lived in the first half of the 2nd century B.C., is known to have been connected with Rhodes. According to Pliny, one of his most famous works was in the sanctuary of the Lindian Athene, and the inscription to it has been excavated since. It says: "During the term of office of Nicagoras, son of Panaetios, as priest of the Lindian Athene, this offering was dedicated to the Lindian Athene by the maker, Boethos son of Athenaeos of Chalcedon, consul and by adoption son of Aenesidamos; Nicagoras, a priest at about 184 B.C., was the father of the famous stoic philosopher, Panaetios. But neither Pliny nor the inscription give any hint as to what that work was; it might have been a large, engraved silver bowl, or some statue of the type above referred to—both would be regarded as engraver's work by the ancients. Engraving was on the whole highly appreciated in Rhodes, and famous hammered works by old artists were carefully kept in the city. Such a "Toreut,, e.g. was M y s, the man who had hammered the shield of Pheidias' Athene Promachos upon drawings of Parrasios. There was even a particular type of engraved skyphoi which were known as Rhodian. The philologist Dionysius the Thracian, who was also a painter and, as mentioned earlier, lived in Rhodes, engraved "Nestor's depas,, according to Homer's description (Iliad : L. 632/37) with money collected for that purpose by his students.

But all these other works of art are eclipsed by the N i k e (Victory) o f S a m o t h r a c e, the pride of the Louvre. For, based both on internal and external evidence, it can now be considered almost certain that this is a Rhodian work, and most probably also an offering of Rhodes, perhaps in gratitude to the gods for the victories of their admiral Eudamos in the war against Antiochos in the year 190 B.C. or thereabouts. The technique and style of the statue also point to this period. The marble of the large prow that constitutes the base of the "Victory,, is "Lartian,, i.e. Rhodian, and from the findings of Lindos we know how fond the Rhodians were of ship-shaped bases for their statues. The statue is like a triumphant proclamation of hellenistic baroque, and an organic growth deeply rooted in its period. "In the foaming waves of form that wash over the statue on all sides, in the impetus of the body which is full of energy, and in its multiple movement, a new image of the goddess of victory is born, an image that has indeed the primeval force of the cosmic element,, (Buschor); but the absolute coincidence of conception and execution·and the unique freshness of the "Victory,, transcend time and elevate it to the category of eternal masterpieces. It would certainly be interesting to know its creator. But there is hardly any evidence to confirm the hypothesis —advanced not wholly without justification by some authorities— that the artist who made the "Victory,, was P y t h o- c r i t o s, son of Timocharis, a Rhodian known from several signatures on works of art, including the prow upon a rock found in Lindos, which had also been the base of a statue (page 46 and pl. 60).

P h i l i s k o s was a Rhodian sculptor of note. Several works by him are mentioned,

*The Nike of Samothrace (Louvre)*

including a group of statues representing the 9 Muses, which were subsequently transported to Rome, and must date from about the same period as the many copies in relief or statue form, possibly also his, that have been preserved. "The main features of this composition are the sequence of a variety of graceful postures, and the intricate details of the dress, masterfully contrasting the transparent and silkily soft himatia with the sumptuously heavy drapes of the chitons beneath,,. This style which underlines the feminine curves of the bodies was prevalent around the middle of the 2nd century, and some fine examples of it can be seen in the museum of Rhodes.

The "Victory,, testifies to the high quality standards of the hellenistic art in Rhodes. It would then seem not unlikely to infer the Rhodians' participation in that other great artistic creation of the period, which is the plastic decoration of the famous "a l t a r   o f   P e r g a m o n,,. On the other hand, we cannot affirm such participation with objective certainty, nor draw from it any conclusions concerning the particular artistic trends in Rhodes, until it has been proved that Menekrates, one of the artists who made the reliefs and possibly also the architect of the altar, is the same as the stepfather of two artists from Tralleis of Asia Minor who are certain to have worked in Rhodes, and who signed their works : "A p o l l o n i o s   a n d   T a u r i s k o s, sons of Artemidoros, and by adoption sons of Menekrates, Trallians,,. These are the authors of a group representing Zethos and Amphion about to punish Dirce for having tortured their mother Antiope, and tying her to the horns of a wild bull who would tear her to pieces as he ran raging on Mt. Cithaeron.

An idea —a very poor one— of this group can be obtained from a Roman, heavily overdone copy of the 2nd century A.D., kept in the museum of Naples and known as the "Farnese Bull,,; more than half of this copy was added in a subsequent period. The original Rhodian group included only Zethos, Amphion, Dirce, and the bull, "all made out of one single stone,, (ex eodem lapide) as reported by Pliny. The original must have been made around 100 B.C. and was probably taken away and sent to Rome by Cassius in 42 B.C. It would have been more closely knit than the very loosely connected Roman copy, and its craftsmanship would have been superior. A much more accurate impression of the quality of hellenistic art is conveyed by a small statue of a nymph sitting on a rock, her posture and the way she wears the himation looking almost like a contemporary copy of the original Dirce. This statue is now in the Museum of Rhodes and it has rightly been suggested that it must have come out of the same workshop of Apollonios and Tauriskos in Rhodes (pl. 25).

A preference for literary and tragic themes is unmistakably present in this work, as well as in Laokoon, to be discussed later; this is indeed a general trend in the late period of hellenistic art and perhaps more markedly so in Rhodes. It is present also in the bronze group by Aristonidas, a sculptor of probably the 2nd century B.C., a descendant of an old family of Rhodian artists. The group represented the legendary king of Orchomenos, Athamas, just after he had killed his son Learchos in a burst of rage, and was now repenting his rash act. To show the blush of shame on his cheeks, the artist blended the bronze with iron, whereby oxidation caused the metal to take on a suggestive hue. At the time of Pliny (2nd half of the 1st century B.C.) the work was still in Rhodes. We do not know, however, whether, apart from this technical trick, it had intrinsic value as a work of art.

On 14th January 1506, under the wonder-filled eyes of the architect Giulano da San Gallo and his friend Michelangelo, a Rhodian masterpiece saw the light of Rome : the group of L a o k o o n and his two sons being killed by two huge serpents. The group was already famous in antiquity. Pliny, who saw it at Titus' palace in Rome, described it as "superior to all other works of painting and bronze sculpture,,, adding, in his admiration, that the statues of the three men, and "the wonderful loops of the snakes,, were all of one piece of marble (ex uno lapide) —which is not correct as the group actually is made up of four blocks of marble. To Pliny too, we owe the names of the artists : they were the three Rhodians P o l y d o r o s, A t h e n o d o r o s and A g e s a n d r o s. The first is otherwise unknown, but we do have some information about the others from inscriptions found at Lindos. They were brothers and one of them, Athenodoros, son of Agesandros, by adoption son of Dionysios, was already active as a sculptor in 42 B.C., and became priest of the Lindian Athene in 22 B.C. The other, Agesandros son of Agesandros, by adoption son of Damaenetos, also became a priest in 21 B.C. It is likely that this double honour was a reward for their making of the Laokoon group, probably a few years earlier, certainly in Rhodes, since the base was repaired with Rhodian marble by decision of the town council (de consilii sententia). Later, the Rhodians presented it to emperor Titus, either when he stopped at Rhodes in 69 A.D., or when he gave them back their freedom in 79 A.D.

The enthusiasm of later generations, from the Renaissance onwards about this group, seems exaggerated at present. Especially the former poor restoration of the right arms of Laokoon and his son, at the Vatican, emphasized excessively the diagonal movement of the group as a whole. But also the composition of the group, now almost reduced to a relief, with regard to the interrelation of its parts as well as to the presentation of the bodies and to the expression of pain, conveys an impression of cold calculation, a lacking of genuine hellenistic feeling, and a tendency to classicism. It is "an academic piece of bold craftsmanship, where all reserves of the skill of composition, of anatomical knowledge obtained from dead bodies, of psychological effects, have been used. Only one who has felt deep in his being all the mortal cold, the separation of limbs which were previously linked together in the rhythm of life, can do justice to such a work. Then, this dying priest can become the symbol of the profound changes occurring in that period,, (Buschor). However, it is certain that later artists of the caliber of a Titian, a Michelangelo, a Rubens were strongly and permanently influenced by this entirely new kind of art. Michelangelo indeed is known to have refused to repair the work for fear he might be unable to come up to the quality of the original. He is also said to have been intensely concerned with the problem of the body writhing in its desperate struggle to liberate itself from its earthen bonds. It has been said that Laokoon, not Michelangelo, is the true father of the new baroque.

In the Roman Period, artistic and intellectual activity decline, just as political and economic activity had declined earlier. There is no abrupt stop in artistic production: but the inner drive is gone, and works springing from a desire for expression become ever rarer; the motives of artistic production become more and more external. The sanctuaries, public squares and streets, are still teeming with statues : According to Pliny, there were more than 3.000 statues in Rhodes in 60 A.D. This is again confirmed at the time of

*Laocoon Group (Vatican museum).*

Titus (abt. 80 A.D.) by the orator Dion Chryssostomos, who said in a speech to the Rhodians: "There is nothing you enjoy more than a multitude of statues,,. But the context in which this phrase occurs is illuminating : Dion blames the Rhodians for their habit to honour any new benefactor by taking any old statue and just changing the name of the person honoured thereby. This is additional evidence of the fact that the world of art still surrounding the Rhodians no longer has the throb and warmth of creativeness, but is something of the past that belongs to "history,, and is venerated as such.

This brief account includes only a small part of the large number of names, works, and historical incidents mentioned in the sources, to say nothing of the great variety of monuments kept at various museums and not counting all the information derived from inscriptions about the artists, both Rhodians and aliens, who worked in Rhodes, and about Rhodian artists who worked elsewhere. A recent list of artists known from inscriptions of Rhodes published so far, includes upward of 100 names in the last four centuries B.C., with more than one work attributed to some of them. But perhaps the best testimony for the deep roots of artistic tradition and for its genuineness and spontaneity is that, as far as we know, Rhodes was the only place —not even excluding classical Athens— where artists enjoyed a high social standing. In the Hellenistic Period at least, it is obvious from many inscriptions that the artists were held in high esteem within the Rhodian society. The city appointed them to the highest religious and political offices; it was easier here than in any other place for an alien artist to become, both legally and actually, a citizen. Together with their innate love of art, this certainly contributed to the sons of artists sticking to their fathers' occupation. There were families in Rhodes consisting of successive generations of artists for many centuries. It is obvious that such circumstances contribute to the maintenance of a high standard of the average artistic production.

### Middle Ages and the Modern Era

In the late centuries of antiquity and in the early years of the Christian Era, information about the arts and artists of Rhodes is scarce. The tradition of craftsmanship, however, while undergoing a change, was never obliterated; witness the monuments of the new religion which turn up or are identified now and again. In the 6th century A.D., the name of Rhodes is mentioned again, in connection with the earliest and greatest architectural achievement of modern times : St. Sophia. When Justinian had the church built in 532-537, the clay bricks for the dome—the boldest element in the new architecture— were ordered from Rhodes; these bricks had to be of very large size, but they also had to be very carefully made so that they should all have the same weight and size. When the dome was damaged and had to be repaired a few years later, the bricks again came from Rhodes. This seems to confirm that the Rhodian craftsmen, at least in some types of work, had not lost their reputation.

As is the case with political history, and for similar reasons, specific events or names connected with the cultural history of the Middle Ages and of the beginnings of the Modern Era, are few, and their sequence is obscure.

Both from these and from present realities, however, it is evident that the end of antiquity did not mark the end of the Greek culture of Rhodes, and that the latter never lost its continuity or its ability to create new living forms.

It has been said about the modern Greek language and its evolution in the Middle Ages that "while the scholars, adhering to the immortal master-pieces of the ancestors, were trying to preserve the forms of the past and especially language, which is a form embodying all others —the forgotten people, by a return to nature, was taking apart the sophisticated organiza-tion of the ancient tongue, and from its debris, and from foreign elements, it was building the new language in a quiet continuous process, always pro-gressing, until the new language came up and dominated all the classes of society ... the true Greek character consists in its aliveness, in the beautiful simplicity of its form and in the clarity of its depth,, (Polylas). These words describe very well the manifestations and the results of the change, even if they do not describe its inner processes. They are true, with the necessary modi-fications, of all the manifestations of civilization, and of all parts of Greece; but they are more particularly true of Rhodes, and other islands, because of the peculiarities of their historical development. For the purposes of this discussion, the general cultural level and the anonymous popular creations are of at least equal, if not greater, importance as the names and works of specific scholars, which may, after all, be considered accidental, especially when they do not fit into the general picture.

Such names, however, are not missing. In the 10th century, for example, a well-known scholar was C o n s t a n t i n   t h e   R h o d i a n from Lindos he went to Constantinople to complete his studies, and there he became first a "grammarian,,, and later, around 920 A.D. a member of the "royal clergy,, in the Court of Constantin Porphyrogennetos. Apart from other poems, he wrote a description in iambic verse, of the Church of the Holy Apostles of Con-stantinople which provides useful information about this important and no longer extant church. It is interesting to note that though the poet misses no opportunity to express his scorn of the religion of the ancient Greeks and of their statues, including his former compatriots of Lindos for their worship of Athene, he does reproduce an ancient epigram from the acropolis of Lin-dos, where one of its last priests, Aglochartos of the 3rd or 4th century A.D., speaks of the olive trees he had planted in the sacred precinct of the goddess. It is a moving fact, that this ancient epigram, which is recorded in the 15th book of the Palatine Anthology together with various other epigrams by this Byzantine scholar, also relating to Lindos, under the heading "In the castle of Lindos at the western promontory,, has been found and can be read today on the western side of the rock of the Lindian Athene.

Names of Rhodian scholars, of greater or lesser significance, who developed their activity in Rhodes or elsewhere, have come down to us from almost all centuries of the Byzantine and the Modern Era. But there is also sufficient evidence to suggest that the av-erage cultural level of Rhodes was by no means insignificant. An important cultural centre in nearby Patmos was the monastery of St. John Theologos with a large library and a fa-mous set of "codices,,. A similar secondary cultural centre seems to have been established in Rhodes, at the old monastery of St. John Theologos situated at Artamites on one of the southeastern hills of the central Mt. Atabyrion; this monastery was founded in the 9th or 10th century A.D. and had also a considerable library. The monk and writer of Constantinople Nikephoros Vlemmydes (1198-1272), who had developed important activity in Nicaea and Ephesos came to Rhodes in the time of its semi-independent ruler Gavalas and spent several months at this monastery. Many manuscripts of the Library of Patmos, and other libraries, were written by Rhodian scholars, sometimes even by "cavallieri,, with a knowledge of Greek, such as a codex of verses by the Cretan Stephanos Sachlikis. The same impression is given later by a text by the Florentine abbot Christopher Buondelmonti, who lived in Rhodes for 8 years, acquired a good knowledge of ancient Greek and in 1420 A.D. wrote a book describing his travels, under the title : "Liber insularum,,.

Another representative of the late Byzantine scholars who, without having completely shaken off the scholastic tradition, were unable to resist the beneficial influence of the quantitatively and qualitatively rapidly rising vernacular, was the verse-writer E m m a n u e l  G e o r g i l a s in the last decade of the rule of the Knights. One of the writings which are certainly his, "Historical account of Velissarios,, deals with an old Byzantine subject in an almost pure demotice; a more vital and culturally significant of his works is "The Epidemic of Rhodes,,; it refers to the then recent epidemic of 1498-9, is written in political rhyming verse, but its heavily didactic tone rarely allows any true-ringing feeling to come through.

Of incomparably higher aesthetic value are the f o l k  s o n g s, most of which have survived to this day. As far as the historical origins of these songs are concerned, it is certainly no coincidence, e.g. that the verses wherewith the children of many parts of Greece including Rhodes greet the arrival of the swallows in March, have their counterpart in the ancient Lindian "swallow-song,,, which has been attributed to Kleoboulos, but has all the characteristics of a true folk song. We have more accurate information about the date of a series of very fine love-songs. The manuscript —now in the British Museum, in which they have been preserved under the title "K a t o l o g i a —verses of love and affection,, belongs to the 2nd half of the 15th century A.D., and the songs themselves cannot be much older. They are a good example of medieval folk songs i.e. of the folk songs of a period when the Greek and the Western world, on the eve of the Renaissance, had already established direct and fruitful contacts. The songs were formerly considered Rhodian. Scholars today are less certain and would rather broaden the area of their origin to include the whole Dodecanese, including Rhodes. The few external pieces of evidence associating them with Rhodes maintain their significance. The particular atmosphere of the songs, reflecting the meeting of two worlds and the relaxation of the old social structures is certainly well fitted to the Rhodes of the Cavallieri. The freshness and clarity of their form are values belonging to the people that created these poems:

> *You are a crimson column in the palace where the king*
> *dwells and the judge administers justice, our lady's*
> *image, and the king's most precious possession, the honour*
> *of princes and the glory of rulers.*
> *You are the cool of the night and the dew of winter,*
> *the glow of sunset and the light of day, the lucifer*
> *of dawn and the lamp keeping the palace from darkness.*
> *You are a star in the sky, a flower in the plain,*

*a much-envied land of great wealth.*
*Of the sun's crown of rays you are one,*
*Of Adam's ribs you are one,*
*Of those that inflame and burn hearts with love you are one,*
*Of nightingales singing you are one.*

When Rhodes was taken by the Turks in 1522 A.D., its cultural level was comparable to that of Crete, but Crete was able to maintain its culturally fertile contacts with the west for another century and a half, until it also fell to the Turks in 1669 A.D.

As to the arts after antiquity, there is perhaps enough information concerning "art in Rhodes,,, but the "a r t   o f   R h o d e s,, has not yet been adequately investigated and documented, with the exception of the architecture of the period of the Knights. The monuments of early Christian and Byzantine art are only just being discovered, or identified and studied. From the period of the Knights and from later years, we find some very fine carved furniture, and woven articles expressing popular aesthetic concepts modified by external influences of as yet unidentified purport. The same is true of architecture in the period of Turkish rule. Most of the fine ceramics known as R o d i t i k a   or   p l a t e s   o f   L i n d o s   are found in other places as well. They date from the 15th - 16th century and are adorned with colourful decorations, mainly with vegetal, sometimes animal or human forms (fig. p. 95).

Current opinion is that these were not made locally but came from the workshops of Asia Minor (Nicaea, Kioutachia, etc.), and indeed theirs is the common decorative language of the oriental world of the period, believed to be of Persian origin. It is possible, however, that careful study may shed some more light not only on their decorative themes, but also on their style in a broader sense, i.e. their function and their greater or lesser adaptation to the environment, and so differentiate them and possibly discern more specific western or Greek trends in these ceramics, some of which are reminiscent of old Rhodian potteries.

# THE MONUMENTS OF RHODES

The outermost NE promontory of the island, the ancients "Pan's end,,, terminates at the sandy projection of Koum-Bournou; it is separated from the inland to the west and to the south by a soft and not very tall hill range. These hills form the boundary of a fairly large triangular plain which is open to the sea on the north and east, and kept always green by adundant waters. This is where the town of Rhodes was built in 408 B.C. and where it stands to this day. It was the harbours that first attracted the people to this area, and this is what still keeps them there. On the eastern side of the triangle, three harbours adjacent to one another open to the sea, all looking north : the first and smaller is M a n d r a k i (pl. 29), next to it farther south is the larger E m b o r i ó, and last is the bay of A k a n d i a.

In the midst of a world of greenery and flowers, the town forms a picture dominated by the peculiar architectural design of the Castle, that is the small walled medieval city, in the front plane, surrounded and beautifully kept apart, by the Turkish and Jewish cemeteries. Farther into the interior of the plain, south, west, and north of the Castle, spacious new residential districts —"m a r a s s i a,, as the Rhodians call the suburbs of their town—are spreading inland (for these, and the following description, refer to fig. p. 91).

The medieval town, wonderfully preserved to this day, almost untouched by time, lends the whole picture a strangeness —for unlike western Europe, these parts have preserved few such complexes of the Byzantine or Latin period. The architectural design of the old city and its parts is of European origin, because it is in fact l a t e  G o t h i c with only slight modifications. But as it is a genuine creation of its time, naturally and spontaneously built and used by its first occupants for their purposes—in a period when the Greek and the western world were very near to each other and their sense of beauty was alike in many things — the Castle of the Knights does not clash with its typically Greek and insular environment, but rather enhances it by adding a novel and unusual flavour.

This is unfortunately not true of the modern buildings of the Italian occupation, erected to the north of the Castle on the seaside by Mandraki and higher up, such as the new market-place, the law-courts, the post-office, the Roman Catholic church of St. John of the Knights (now dedicated to the Annunciation of the Virgin), the Governor's residence, the offices of the harbour authority, the "Hotel of the Roses,, etc. The Italians, with their

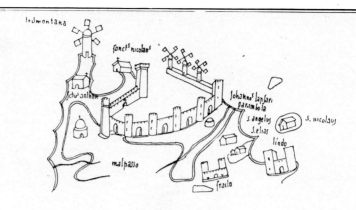

passion for architecture and their tendency to melodramatic forms of expression, did display a sense of space, but failed to achieve harmony between the buildings and a given form of life. They erected buildings calculated to surprise the viewer, to overwhelm the "vassal", to create, within a living environment that did not conform with their purposes, a relation of artificial continuity with the period of the Knights, which they attempted to put down as part of their own history; so they deliberately copied various old styles, mainly Italian, in these presumptuous buildings whose lack of proportion and whose gaudiness are alien even to the medieval city of the Castle and jar like a false note in the scenery. "Let us not talk of them, just cast a look and pass on".

Ancient Rhodes must have looked quite different. Not the natural scenery, of course. The tall palms, typical of all island sanctuaries of Apollo, must have stood there just as they stand now. The architectural framework, however, must have had different outlines and structures. To begin with, the city was certainly much larger. Only fragments of the ancient walls have been unearthed, nor has their exact position been identified with any certainty. The few known remains, however, suggest that the fortified line surrounding the ancient city, partly leaned upon the hills and partly enclosed them (included were for instance the whole of the western hill of St. Stephanos, and, possibly, part of the southwestern Kijil-Tepé); then the wall continued due north but turned east somewhere before it reached the projection and met the seashore in the vicinity of the present Governor's residence; thus both the small harbour (today's Mandraki) and the large harbour (today's Emborió) would be protected, whereas the bay of Akandia does not seem to have been important to the ancients, nor for that matter to any of the subsequent generations down to our times. Another wall also protected the coastline of the main harbours and joined the northern and the southern end of the enclosure.

The area enclosed by the fortified wall is about 700 hectars. Note, for comparison, that the area within the walls of the medieval town of the Castle is only 48 hectars and the population living within that area is 7-8,000. The population of the ancient city in the time of its prime in the 3rd and 2nd century B. C. is estimated at 60-80,000 up to 100,000 according to some estimates.

Within this area, the ancient city was built in a way that aroused the

*St. Nicholas' tower (Gabriel).*

admiration of the ancients : "We cannot tell of any other city that is its equal, much less its superior,, writes Strabo. The hypothesis that its architect was the famous Hippodamos of Miletus does not seem convincing. But it was built in the "Hippodamean,, style, i.e. according to a predetermined geometric design, based on a system of wide streets climbing in straight lines from the east (from the harbours) to the west, and from north to south (inland) cutting each other at regular angles. Built in such a way and surrounded by the southern and western hills, it looked like the "koilon,, of an ancient theatre divided by tiers ("theatre-like,, structure, Diodosor).

At one time, 316 B. C., this structure became the cause of unexpected disaster. Heavy spring rains brought down large amounts of water, which flowed along the streets to the lower part of the city near the harbour and was trapped there because the wall did not allow it to escape and the sewage system was clogged. The resulting flood was terrible; it covered the "Deigma,,, the "Dionysion,, and continued rising toward the Asklepeion; terrified, some of the inhabitants boarded the ships, others ran up to the theatre, still others climbed on high altars and statue pedestals. Finally the water with its terrific weight broke the wall and emptied itself into the sea, but more than 500 persons perished.

The course of most of the ancient streets especially those outside the Castle has not changed essentially, but inside the Castle too, the famous "street of the Knights,, for example is built on one of the ancient streets.

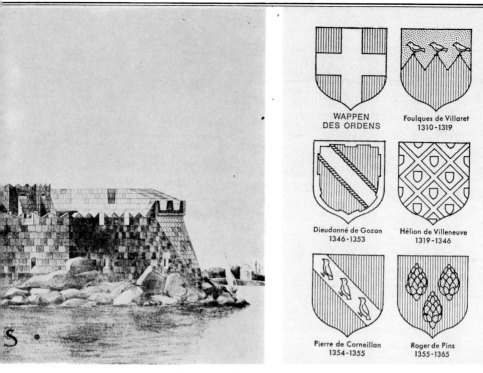

WAPPEN DES ORDENS

Foulques de Villaret 1310-1319

Dieudonné de Gozon 1346-1353

Hélion de Villeneuve 1319-1346

Pierre de Corneillan 1354-1355

Roger de Pins 1355-1365

*The coats of arms of the Great Magisters of Rhodes.*

On the other hand, we know very little about the main buildings and their sequence.

As we are informed by a Latin traveller who visited Rhodes in 1190 A.D., most of the ancient buildings still stood in the late Byzantine Period. But the boundless building activity of the Knights during their 2 centuries on the island was lethal not only to the marble overstructures but to the very foundations of the ancient buildings. So today we know only the names of several important ancient buildings, we know or can deduce where a few of them were situated, and we have some pitiful remains of a very few of them.

The ancient city had two a c r o p o l e i s within its walls : one was high up on top of St. Stephanos' hill, the western side of which falls abruptly down to the sea; the other, a secondary one, was situated much lower, near the harbours, and is the same as the northern part of the Castle, the part referred to as "Castello„ or "Collachio„ in the Middle Ages, and separated from the rest of the Castle by the " B a z a a r   s t r e e t „.

The harbours were naturally a matter of great ‚concern; on the side of the sea, they were protected by solid piers, parts of which can be seen today in the moles of St. Nicholas and Myloi; the northernmost smaller harbour (Mandraki) could also be secured by chains, so this was probably where the war ships were kept. In addition to the "large„ and the "small„ harbour, the ancients mentioned several other harbours "good for any weather,„, but these have probably been covered with alluvial mud and can

Raymond Béranger
1365-1374

Robert de Juilly
1374-1377

Ferdinand d'Hérédia
1377-1396

Philibert de Naillac
1396-1421

*The Mandraki (Caoursin).*

no longer be seen today. The famous Rhodian "dockyards„ which were large dry docks with ware-houses for ship riggings, entrance to which was prohibited on pain of death, must have been at Mandraki.

Near the harbour was the "D e i g m a„ (display centre) where specimens of all kinds of merchandise were on display to facilitate wholesale transactions; here also the bankers and money-changers had their places of business, and the area was adorned with statues, such as the group showing the demos (city) of Syracuse crowning the demos of Rhodes. The market-place must have been located near the "Deigma„. In its vicinity was also the s a n c- t u a r y o f D i o n y s o s (Dionysion), famous for the large number of works of arts it contained. Some ruins found on the northern side of the medieval castle may have belonged to the Dionysion.

On the NE side of the Castle are the ruins of a t e m p l e   t o   A p h r o- d i t e . The sanctuary of the greatest god of Rhodes, H e l i o s, is almost certain to have stood within the area of the medieval Castle, near the ruined church of St. John of the Knights and the palace of the Great Magister, that is within the lower ancient acropolis.

On the hillside of the upper acropolis, i.e. of St. Stephanos' hill, the S t a- d i u m of ancient Rhodes was discovered, as well as a small theatre. The G y m n a s i u m which was as famous as the Dionysion for its works of art must have been around here. Higher up around the acropolis and near the exterior wall stood the g r e a t   T h e a t r e and the t e m p l e   o f  I- s i s, both of which excavations have failed to bring to light so far. Some ruins of the temples o f  A t h e n e   P o l i a s and Z e u s   P o l i e u s as well as of the great t e m p l e   o f   A p o l l o   P y t h i o s have been found in the acropolis on St. Stephanos' hill. In the plain separating the upper from the lower acropolis was the A s k l e p e i o n and the P r y t a n e i o n (behind the barracks) i.e. the headquarters of the highest executive authority (the Prytaneis), possibly also the B o u l e u t e r i o n and other public build- ings.

No detailed description of the city (of the type of Pausanias' descriptions) has been preserved. However, an oration attributed to Ailios Aristides and written to encourage Rhodians to rebuild their city after the 155 A. D. earthquake, provides, despite the rhet- orical bombast, quite a vivid picture of the ancient city. After referring with enthusiasm to the harbours and monuments of the city, it goes on: "You could see the acropolis with its many flat spaces and groves; and in the rest of the city, no part projected above the others, but all were equal and so linked with one another that you would think they were parts not of a town but of a single house. And streets, all straight from beginning to end that deserved anything but the name of lanes. And the splendid town, spreading bril- liantly away on all sides. But the first and foremost wonder that the eyes could not be sated with watching was the circle of the walls and their high and beautiful towers, looking straight as candles to those approaching from the sea—so Rhodes was the only place where men's minds became bigger by just looking at them as they were coming up with the ships. And the nicest of it all was that the circle was not detached from the city nor left any emp- ty space in between, but hugged it tightly on all sides as a crown fits around the head,,. This last simile will be better understood if one remembers that cities to the ancients were almost human, and that they were always represented as women with a crenellated wall for a diadem.

In the following tour will be described, in that order 1) The medieval town enclosed within the Castle of the Knights; 2) the walls of the Castle; 3) the new town outside the Castle.

## 1. The Castle (Castro) or Chora

The walled medieval town C a s t r o (Castle) built in an almost perfect semi-circle around the central harbour Emborió, was divided —as can be clearly seen today— into two unequal parts. The southern and larger part was the C h o r a (bourg-borgo)· proper and in the period of the Knights it was inhabited by the Greeks, the families of Latin laymen, and the Jews (the Jewish quarter was then as now situated at the eastern end).

During the Turkish occupation all Christians were evicted from the Castle, only Turks and Jews being allowed to remain; the market place was also always there.

The northern and smaller section of the Castle which began approximately from the road of the old market, was separated from the other by its own separate wall and so formed a kind of inner acropolis (very near the location of the ancient lower acropolis, some parts of which have been found); this section was called " C a s t e l l o „ or " C o l l a c h i o „.

The "Castello„ was reserved exclusively for the Knights, and here were the most important buildings connected with the religious and the worldly life of the Order : the palace of the Great Magister, the hospital, etc. A special group of buildings within this inner "Castello„ were the so-called "I n n s „ (Auberges of the various ethnic groups of which the Order was composed, and whose official designation was "tongues„. Each of these groups or tongues was in charge of a determined part of the wall which it had to guard, and had, within the Castello, an inn i.e. a smaller or larger house, a kind of club, where the members of the group had their midday and evening meals, and which served also as a residence for the group's officials (abbot, prior) and as a guest-house for important visitors. Most of the "inns„ have been preserved and are adequately identified.

The architectural aspect of the Castle has remained essentially unchanged since the time of the Knights. The houses and the churches of Chora as well as the more splendid buildings of the "Castello„ are the same, and so are the streets. The Turks added few new buildings —especially for religious purposes— and changed the old buildings very little, for the most part just adding lattice-windows to houses or minarets to churches turned into mosques. Even these few changes have been mostly eliminated in the last years, after the Second World War, and all the most important medieval buildings have been restored to their original form. The main features of this medieval town were determined by the Gothic architectural style in the form which was prevalent in Provence (the Great Magisters of Rhodes were closely related with the Papal Court of Avignon, 1309-1424), in Spain and Italy.

In these countries, however, there was in that period an increasing trend toward the late Gothic variety known as "flamboyant„; the Gothic style of Rhodes is more conservative and austere, as befitted the religious and monastic, as well as military character of the Order. Here both the great palaces of the Knights and the churches are impressive by their volume, imposingly dominating space, but they are almost bare; their surfaces are hardly linked to the —few— doors and windows, and architectural decoration is sparse. It should be pointed out, however, that north-western architecture, both in its romanesque and its Gothic form, always made buildings look "militant„, combative, in the face of the uncertain community, and made the façades even of the churches look like faces "glaring at the enemy„ (Pinder).

The large urban houses of the Knights display the following general features: The ground floor was all taken up by large store-rooms (magasins) around an inner courtyard. The front had a series of large arches, not always of the same shape, giving access to the store-rooms on the side of the street, and to the inner courtyard. In the upper floors, which served as living quarters and for other uses, the front was distinguishable from that of the ground-floor only by the different spacing of the windows. So the façade, especially of the older buildings, is a uniform surface in which not even the centre is particularly underlined — as even front doors which did differ by their form, were usually placed off to one end— nor are there any lines indicating the division of floors. On the whole, the façade reveals nothing of the internal arrangement of rooms. A certain organization of the façade is achieved by the deliberate arrangement of doors and windows. Though the effect is often quite aesthetic, this style is not "organic,,, in the sense that it is not dictated by functional requirements (as classical architecture, both ancient and modern, is) but aims only at making the façade more interesting, i. e. it is purely decorative (the term is not used here in any derogatory sense). Only around 1500, do we find in Rhodes any signs of the new style of the Renaissance which had begun in Italy more than a century earlier, and only then can a new trend be detected in the aspect of the façades.

Scholars concerned with the study of the architectural history of Rhodes, divide it into two very unequal periods. During the first of these periods, 1308-1480, the new buildings of the Knights are supposed to have been constructed by local craftsmen, accustomed to other kinds of work, to other styles, and this explains why the early Gothic works of this period, apart from retaining a certain amount of Byzantine influence, are of inferior craftsmanship compared with corresponding works in the west. In 1480, the siege by Mohamed II caused severe damage to the town, compounded later by the great earthquake of 1481. The Great Magister D'Aubusson (1476-1503), a noteworthy personality, had almost to rebuild the town and the walls, a task to which he applied himself with great energy.

This marks the beginning of a second period (lasting until the fall of Rhodes to the Turks in 1522) to which belong —in their original or repaired form — almost all important buildings in the Castle, as well as the walls. This time the work was done by architects and craftsmen specially brought over from the west. This is the reason why, these works are supposed to be more uniform in their conception and execution, and of higher aesthetic value. This division, however, appears rather artificial. Evidence of considerable participation of local craftsmen consists of certain works, inscriptions, as well as of the fact that many Greek technical terms, the jargon of artists and craftsmen, occur repeatedly in the pertinent manuscripts of the Knights, though these were drafted in foreign languages. Whatever the case may be, the fact remains that the contact between Greek and western artistic trends and its results has still to be studied in its essence and from the positive point of view.

Tour: We begin from the northern section of the Castle, which is the internal acropolis of the Knights, the medieval "Castello,, or "Collachio,,. Most of the more magnificent buildings of the Knights are concentrated in this area. The term "Castello,, is often used to denote the palace of the Great Magister specifically. In this description, we use the name in its medieval sense, that is in contrast to the southern section of the Castle, or Chora. The numerals refer to the topographic plan on pages 134-135.

### a) Castello or Collachio

Coming from the seashore of "Mandraki,,, we enter through the new G a t e  o f  F r e e d o m (made in 1924) into the A r s e n a l  S q u a r e, so called because it was believed that this is where the Knights had their shipyards. From this square, the A r s e n a l  G a t e on the left leads to the harbour of Emborió. In the front part of the square are the remains of the small t e m p l e  t o  A p h r o d i t e (pl. 45), identified by means of some vo- tive offerings and two inscriptions. Preserved are the foundations and a few architectural parts, such as column bases and drums, some fragments of the epistyle; these suggest that the temple was originally built in the 3rd century B.C., but was subsequently repaired on several occasions. The cult of Aphrodite was common in seaside places (Euploia, Limenia, Pontia).

In the background stands the ponderous I n n  o f  t h e  T o n g u e  o f  A u v e r g n e (plan I, 1), a building dating from the 15th century, and com- pleted in 1507. From the ground floor, which houses the store-rooms, three broad arches open onto the square. At the right-hand corner, a staircase (with a bend) leads up to a gallery (loggia) with four arches at the front; this is the entrance to the first floor, which was the living quarters (hearths from the time of the Knights are preserved within). The façade bears no ornamen- tation other than the effect created by the alternation of levels resulting from the projecting gallery, the varying span of the arches and the mutual propor- tions of the various parts. The staircase attached to the façade (rather than in the courtyard or to a side wall) is a feature appearing in some of the other buildings as well, and is an Aegean —not western— architectural element.

The atmosphere changes abruptly if, turning to the right and going past the heaps of large stone balls (supposed to have been gathered for use during the siege of 1522; similar heaps can be seen in other parts of the Castle as well), we proceed to a small square in front of a large building now housing the H i s t o r i c a l - A r c h a e o l o g i c a l  I n s t i t u t e (plan I, 2), but formerly used by the Turks, and possibly also by the Knights, as an a r m o u r y. (Armeria). It is an austere structure, one of the oldest in the Castle since it dates from the 14th century (the loggia to the left of the entrance is a modern addition). The original shape and arrangement of the rooms of the first floor, similar to that of the great Hospital of the Knights (Museum), suggest that this may have been the o l d  h o s p i t a l built by the Great Magister R. De Pins (1355-1365); his coat of arms together with that of the Order can be seen at the right hand side of the façade; when the new hospital was built, the old one was converted for other purposes, the internal arrangement was adjusted and at the left hand corner of the outside where the apse of the Gothic chapel of the hospital had been, they opened a front door in the years of the Great Magister Del Carretto (1513-1521, coat of arms over the door); the pointed door-frame as well as the two pointed narrow windows on either side are remains of the chapel. The gloomy façade strongly reminiscent of a tower, is divided, by means only of the vertical raws of openings and of the shape of the roof, into three parts : on the left, the part including the front door, ends above at the horizontal raw of crenellations, while the two parts on the right end at two very wide triangles, the apex of each correspond- ing to both vertical rows of windows below. In this way, a segmentation of the otherwise uniform, strongly Gothic, façade, is achieved (pl. 33).

Following the road going past the western side of the Inn of Auvergne and leading through an arch - roofed passage to the centre of the Castle, we can see, on the left, the main entrance of the Inn of Auvergne, on the southern side of the building. This is a pointed Gothic doorway, framed by bundles of carved bars and, above the arch, by a separate rectangular frame (in this can be seen the coats of arms of the Order and of Guy de Blanchefort, later a Great Magister, and the date 1507); the frames are partly decorated with plant designs. This door, one of the richest and most elegant in the town of the Knights, is similar to those of the Inns of Provence and of France. Continuing along the same street, under various arcades, we presently come before the E n d e r o u m (or Kantouri) mosque (plan I, 3), opposite the beginning of the s t r e e t  o f  t h e  K n i g h t s: this used to be the old Roman Catholic cathedral dedicated to the Virgin Mary (Sainte-Marie du Château), which the Turks converted into a mosque without altering the interior, by merely adding the front gallery with the small domes and substituting a minaret for the old steeple; at the back, the apse of the sanctum leans against the Castello wall. The design is simple, consisting of a cross inscribed in a rectangle; but while the two lower side aisles are covered with a cylindrical vault, the higher central nave has a typical Gothic roof with pointed' cross-vaults, and the apse of the sanctum, which is round up to a point, then becomes polygonal to fit the Gothic roof. It seems likely that this was originally a purely Byzantine church, perhaps of the 13th century, and possibly the church of the Greek Orthodox bishop; upon their arrival the Latins turned it over to the Roman Catholic archbishop, and later, in the 15th century, gave it a partly Gothic appearance by changing the roof of the nave and adding the external abutments to the walls. The narrow pointed windows still had the stained glass panes of the 14th and 15th centuries until the great explosion of 1856.

Immediately after the mosque, we come to the small square in front of the Hospital of the Knights (Museum). To the east of this, there is the I n n  o f  t h e  T o n g u e  o f  E n g l a n d (plan I, 4) built in 1919 in the same place and in the same style as the older inn of 1483; the latter had been completely destroyed some time after the Belgian Rottier saw it and made a drawing of it in 1826.

The western side of the square as well as the beginning of the street of the Knights is taken up by the H o s p i t a l  o f  t h e  K n i g h t s (now the Museum, plan I, 5), an austere, imposing building with long sides and a sober appearance. It was begun in 1440 by the Great Magister De Lastic, with money left for this purpose by his predecessor Fluvian, but was completed in its present form by the Great Magister D'Aubusson (pl. 34).

Its façade and main entrance are on the square. On the ground floor, there are three low-arched openings on each side of the similarly arched entrance leading to the store - rooms; here is also the pointed door of the courtyard, framed with carved bars and decorated with various designs (tracery etc.). The upper floor, on the other hand, without a single opening, presents an uninterrupted and almost bare surface. Only exactly above the main entrance is there a projecting three-sided concha. It is the apse of the chapel we will see in the large room of the first floor; its corners are

*The street of the Knights.*

accentuated with sculptured vertical bars, and high it has three Gothic windows. The second ornamental element consists of two horizontal carved belts extending across the whole length of the long façade, then taking a downward twist and forming a step near the concha, the upper belt actually cutting horizontally across the concha below the windows. The pointed doorway of the ground floor, the concha and the twist of the belts form a middle line which, however, is slightly off-centre. On the middle side of the concha, above the entrance to the ground floor, an inbuilt relief shows two angels beneath the flag of the Order, holding the coat of arms of Fluvian or De Lastic, and below them on a marble scroll, the founding inscription announcing in Latin with Gothic lettering that the Great Magister Fluvian bequeathed 10,000 florins "to build this h o t e l„ (huic xenodochio construendo).

The other façade giving on the street of the Knights is more colourful with its larger number of openings and the more varied arrangement of its elements. The lower belt of the other façade, is continued, dividing the surface in two : on the ground-floor there are the arched openings to the storerooms, while the windows of the first floor are rectangular. At the beginning of the street, the eastern corner which corresponds to the large room of the first floor has a higher roof than the rest of this side, and, corresponding to it, at the western end of the building, the large Gothic gateway to the upper floor, with a richly sculptured pointed flamboyant frame and an additional rectangular frame above, extends up the whole height of both floors.

To the right of this gateway, above an arch-roofed passage are the coats of arms of the Order and of one P. Clouet who, according to the inscription in old French, was the supervisor (commandeur) during the construction of the hospital, completed in 1489 (compli fut lospital tout neuf).

The internal arrangement of the building centers around a large inner courtyard, access to which is possible only through the gateway on the square. A large, two-storied gallery with low-arched openings extends along all four sides of the courtyard; it is roofed on the ground-floor with fine pointed cross-vaults and with semicircular arches on the upper floor. On the southern side, a passage leads to a smaller courtyard. From the large courtyard, a modern broad staircase at the south-eastern corner, leads to the upper floor, but as this cuts abruptly through the arched openings of the gallery, it may be a subsequent addition not included in the original design. The whole length of the eastern side (looking on the square) of the upper floor is taken up by a large hall, the sick-ward (infirmerie); this is divided into two aisles by means of a series of pointed arches, and close to the middle of the eastern wall there is a Gothic chapel, whose three-sided concha we have seen projecting out of the façade on the square. The doors leading to the other rooms are on the other sides of the upper floor gallery. At the northwestern corner of this gallery, there is a staircase leading to the entrance on the street of the Knights. The largest of the rooms on the southern side is also connected to the large sick-ward, and is divided into two parts by means of two arches. A hearth preserved in it suggests that it may have been the d i n i n g - r o o m (refectorium) for the nursing staff.

The general aspect of the building has a marked effect of sober austerity which makes it different and is probably associated with its intended use. The architectural elements and details are late Gothic. But the general type of building is not the one usually found in Frankish hospitals (hôpitaux and "hotels Dieu,,). A large building with many rooms around a central peristyle inner courtyard is the characteristic type of the Byzantine guest-house or inn as well as of the Turkish caravan-serai, which is a continuation of the Byzantine inn. The use of the Greek word "xenodochium,, in the Latin founding inscription, may be significant in this connection. The main purpose of this building of the Knights, however was to provide care for the sick (of both sexes), and possibly for orphans or abandoned children, but not to offer hospitality to the poor in general.

Much ancient material, including integral ancient walls, has gone into the construction of the hospital of the Knights. In the small courtyard e.g., there are three well-preserved thick walls of a rectangular building of Roman origin, and a fourth is probably hidden under the medieval walls.

We now come back to the s t r e e t o f t h e K n i g h t s (pl. 35), which is in itself an imposing medieval monument of a unique purity of character. The street is absolutely straight because coincides with an ancient street leading from the harbour to the acropolis. It is just over 200 m. long and 6 m. wide, and it, too, leads from the harbour to the highest point of the medieval Castle, i.e. to the northwestern corner with the palace of the Great Magister on the right and St. John's church on the left. Most of the major buildings of the Knights look upon this street and lend it its peculiar character. The initial part of the street, on the left, is taken up by the long northern side of the Hospital (now the Museum). On the right, there are first two smaller buildings (the second has a fine rectangular window with a marble grid and a triple frame with carved decorations), followed by the I n n o f t h e T o n g u e o f I t a l y (plan. I, 6) which was completed in 1519 by the Italian Great Magister Del Carretto (his coat of arms can be seen in the middle of the 4 upper floor windows). Its exterior is simple : at the ground floor, a broad low-arched arcade on the left-hand corner leads to the store-rooms, and next to it on the right, a much smaller pointed doorway gives access to the inner courtyard, from where a staircase leads to the upper floor. On the upper floor façade, the horizontal dimension is emphasized by the long straight line of the carved double belt and by the large rectangular windows. The internal arrangement of the rooms may be considered typical of the residences of the Knights.

Next to the Inn of Italy there is a nice small u n i d e n t i f i e d p a l a c e (plan. I, 7), separated into two wings by the two different levels of the roof. The higher left-hand wing includes, below, the pointed entrance gateway, on the first floor, over a carved belt, a pointed double-sloping window, and beside that coats of arms (the middle one of the Great Magister D'Amboise) with the date 1505; the lower, and later, right wing has on the ground floor the low-arched openings of the store-rooms and of a passage leading to the rear, and on the first floor, over a long carved belt, three windows, and three coats of arms in a frame with the date 1521 (the first coat of arms on the right is the Great Magister's De l'Isle-Adam); near the roof there are 4 stone "flagbearing„ rings.

Next to the Hospital (Museum) on the left, another u n i d e n t i f i e d h o u s e (plan I, 8) of late 15th century, probably Spanish, has a door of the so-called "Catalan„ or "Aragon„ type (to be seen again later in the Inn of Spain), consisting of a semicircular arch formed by huge voussoirs.

Across from this, on the right side of the street, stands the I n n o f t h e T o n g u e o f F r a n c e (plan I, 9, pl. 36), the most richly ornamented in this street and one of the loveliest in the town, built in the late years of the 15th century and in the early years of the 16th by the Great Magisters D'Aubusson and D'Amboise. On the ground floor can be seen from right to left: a broad low-arched store-room arch; next to it the beautiful pointed door of the main entrance (to the courtyard, which includes the staircase to the upper floor) which is very similar to the doorway of Auvergne we saw earlier, and to that of Provence nearby, with carved bars at the sides and a rectangular frame over the pointed arch (within the frame, coats of arms of the Order, of D'Amboise and others, with the date 1492); then three more store-room arches and a higher one over the roofed passage leading to the back; the richly ornamented pointed main gateway is not in the centre but off to the righthand corner. Above these openings, running across the whole length of the façade, two carved belts separate the upper from the ground floor. These belts are not straight, but following the rise of the street, twist two or three times and after each twist they proceed at a different level. Similarly, of the 5 windows of the upper floor (all rectangular with a separate frame at the top), the first on the left is at a higher level than the others, and corresponding changes of level can be seen in the four monstrous-like gargoyles of the roof.

The horizontal dimension of the roof —though edentelate with crenellations— restores the unity of line in conjunction with the four semicircular turrets which are distributed at nearly equal intervals along the surface. The first floor façade is dominated by the two windows, coupled by a common ornamented carved frame, and between them, in a separate carved frame, two coats of arms —that of France (three lilies and the royal crown) and that of the Great Magister D'Aubusson (with a cardinal's hat), and the date, 1495. This, too, isslightly off centre. The form of each architectural feature, and these repeated deviations from the vertical and the horizontal axis are typical of the Gothic style (these "twists,, or fractures, for which the Gothic style is fond of have also given the name "Fraktur,,, to the Gothic writing), and divide the whole into several small units, with secret correspondences among them. This, however, is the late period of the Gothic style. The marked emphasis on the horizontal —not the vertical— structure, already announces the rearrangement of elements to be introduced by the Renaissance; in the Inn of France, the result is graceful and elegant.

Adjacent to the Inn of France, in the marble-roofed lane leading to the rear, there is a staircase on the left going up to a doorway with a marble frame in the style of the Renaissance, dated 1510 (plan I, 10); the door posts and the lintel have straight-lined chisel strokes and a rosette each. The anta-capitals of the doorposts resemble Corinthian. Three coats of arms and the date are above. The door opens onto the garden of this house (which appears to be an annex to the Inn of France) and from there a staircase leads to the first floor, which has an interesting façade.

Turning to the right at the end of the lane, we see (on the left) the Gothic chapel of S t. D e m e t r i o s (plan, I, 11) dedicated in 1499 by Louis Piossasco (the Order's admiral); the chapel consists of a single aisle with a pointed arch and an apse which is round on the inside and three-sided on the outside. It is built on the base of the ancient t e m p l e o f D i o n y s o s as witnesses a choragus' inscription at the base of a tripod found in the floor of the church. This then, was probably the ancient D i o n y s i o n, known to have stood in the lower part of the city near the "Deigma,, and the port. It was famous for the many works of art the ancients had accumulated in it.

Here were Protogenes' two famous paintings "Ialyssos,, and "Resting Satyr,,. Here too, around the stoas of the temple, were many paintings relating to the legends of Rhodes, and as (the false) Lucianos says, local guides would explain all the stories to foreigners "for a small fee,,. Several famous hammered works by Akragas and Mys were kept at the temple, and there was a profusion of fine tripods dedicated (as was the custom in Athens), by "choragi,, who had won at the theatrical and musical competitions.

Coming back to the street of the Knights, and always on the right hand side as we proceed upwards, we come, after passing two houses, to a s m a l l c h u r c h (plan I, 12), the front of which forms a toothlike projection, and on this projection, suspended in the air, as it were, stood a small Gothic shrine supported by a carved prop and covered with a finely worked roof; in it would have been kept some small Gothic statuette; the pointed entrance gateway is off to the left and above this are the coats of arms of France, of the Pope, and of England. The interior was changed radically by the Turks, who had converted it to a mosque, the Han - Zadé. On the marble lintel (of a doorway next to the chapel) there are engraved 5 coats of arms in front from left to right: of England, the Great Magister's H. De Villeneuve, of the Order, the Great Magister's D. De Gozon, of England; and 5 more on the inner side: the Order's, the Great Magisters' P. De Corneillan, R. Bérenger, R. De Pins, and one other. The latest of these Great Magisters is Bérenger (1365-73) and it would seem that the little church was built in his time. Then comes a building with a plain façade, probably the residence of the c h u r c h-w a r d e n (Cappelania) (plan I, 13) of the Tongue of France who would also be responsible for the little church just described. In the ground-floor there are two broad store-room arches and between them the coat of arms of one P. Papefust, 1483; on the first floor, above the carved belt, there are two windows with a double-sloping pointed arch and between them, in a cross-shaped frame, the coats of arms of France, of the Great Magister Del Carretto and of one H. Cheron, 1519.

Immediately after, an arch with a room on top spans the whole width of the street, and beyond that, still on the right, comes the I n n  o f  t h e T o n g u e  o f  P r o v e n c e (plan I, 14), a large building, though part of its height was lost at the explosion of 1856. It has a fine Gothic gate, very much like those of the Inns of France and Auvergne, framed with carved bars (plant ornamentations at the springers of the arch), and a separate rectangular frame above. Over the gate, in a cross, there are the coats of arms of the Order, of France, of the Great Magister Del Carretto, and of F. Flotta, abbot of Toulouse, 1518. The sculptured belt of the first floor forms an additional frame for the cross with the coats of arms (pl. 37).

The wide arch extending across the street, divides into two unequal parts the façade of a majestic building on the left side of the street : the I n n  o f t h e  T o n g u e  o f  S p a i n (plan I, 15). The room above the arch belongs to this building. It was built by the Catalan Great Magister Fluvian (1421-37) and added to by D'Amboise (1503-12). The part of the façade before the arch is ornamentally flanked by two tall octagonal pillars reaching up to the roof (but the roof is not well preserved, and we do not know exactly how the pillars terminated). The horizontal but fractured belt of the façade cuts across the pillars; Fluvian's coat of arms appears below the window; the part beyond the arch, which is the larger, has at the ground floor a first low-arched opening giving access to a typical dark lane (the frame above used to show various Spanish coats of arms), followed by a second, semicircular opening of the "Aragon,, type, i.e. with very large voussoirs in the semicircle; this second opening is the entrance to the courtyard, which contains the staircase leading to the upper floor. The upper floor windows are rectangular. The Gothic character of the building is obvious in the composition of the various elements of the façade, especially in the part before the arch, where the vertical dimension is stressed with particular emphasis.

At the end of the street of the Knights, on the left-hand side, there is the base and part of the pier of a now destroyed large pointed Gothic arch, which formed a sort of monumental terminal to this solemn street, as can be seen in old drawings. This arch was the entrance to an angle-shaped gallery (loggia); the northern leg of the gallery included three arches and extended in line with the street, while the eastern leg extended to the left (a few fragments of pillars with capitals can still be seen) and probably joined the apse of St. John's church to be described presently. Above

*The new church of Saint John (now the church of the Virgin of the Annunciation).*

the arches there was a floor with various rooms for the meetings of church officials. Built in the first half of the 15th century, this gallery would have closed off beauti fully the square on which St. John of the Knights stood (in the place of the Turkish school Souleymanje) (plan I, 16). St. John's, dedicated to the Order's patron saint, and the official church of the Knights, was built in the first part of the 14th century and was well preserved until the middle of last century, though it had been converted earlier to a mosque. In 1856, lightning struck the minaret, and the church blew off when a large store of gunpowder long forgotten in its basement, caught fire. The tremendous explosion, apart from other damage, destroyed what had remained of the Gothic gallery, and of the nearby palace of the Great Magister, and killed some 800 people. Its form, however, is known from Rottiers' drawings: it was a small typical Gothic church, externally plain and austere, with the steeple on the western side across from the entrance. Interiorly it was divided into three aisles by two rows of ancient columns. Here, in the floor and along the walls were the graves of the Great Magisters (the gravestones of De Gozon and Orsini are now in the Cluny Museum of Paris together with other monuments of medieval Rhodes; another one or two are in the museum of Rhodes). An exact copy of the medieval St. John's though perhaps a little heavier, is St. John's church built by the Italians at Mandraki by the sea.

At the highest spot of the medieval castle and on the right if one faces the western fortified wall, there stood, across from St. John's church, the Palace of the Great Magister (plan I, 17), a building of the 14th c., imposing by its size (75 × 80 m.) and by its form, and fortified in itself like a separate bastion at the northwestern corner of the Castle. It was ruined to a great extent during the Turkish occupation and the explosion of 1856 had finished its destruction, but it was wholly rebuilt in our time by De Vecchi.

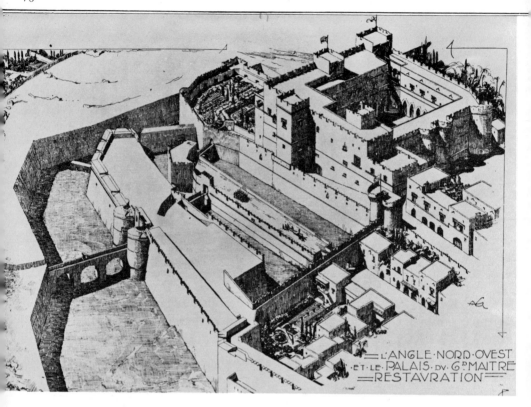

L'ANGLE·NORD·OVEST
·ET·LE·PALAIS·DV·Gᴿ·MAITRE
RESTAVRATION

*The palace of the Great Magister.*

Genuine medieval fragments are the lower part of the outer walls, the main entrance on St. John's square with the large pointed gateway between two round towers and a few parts of the Great Magister's residence on the northeastern side (pls. 29, 41 - 43).

The erection of the new palace upon the remains of the medieval building, and the transportation of a profusion of Hellenistic and Roman mosaics from Kos to decorate its floors, are deplorable acts of megalomania —regardless of the merits or demerits of the work, of its historical accuracy, and its aesthetic value. For logical deduction based on existing information and some inscriptions found in the area, point with near-certainty to this open area of St. John's church and the palace, which was also the most prominent part of the ancient lower acropolis and of all the lower city from the harbours up to he hills, as the site of the famous ancient (perhaps extremely ancient) s a n c t u a r y   o f   H e l i o s  with its rich collection of votive monuments including Lysippos' splendid quadriga and, possibly, connected even with the Colossos. True, the enormous constructions of the Knights would not have left much of the ancient buildings, but at any rate, the area of the church and the palace has never been investigated to any depth.

In this section, which lies well above the level of all the external walls of the Castle, the wall of the inner acropolis, i. e. of the "Castello„ or "Collachio,, is fairly well preserved. The G a t e  o f  t h e  C a n n o n s (top-kapu, plan I, 18), as the Turks used to call it, a gate with a semicircular arch is in this part of the wall, not far from the southwestern corner of the palace of the Great Magister. On the outside, this gateway is flanked by two semi-circular towers which extend down to the moat and are crenellated on top. Above the arch, the coats of arms of the Order and of the Great Magister De Lastic are shown. The Gate of the Cannons is connected by a pont-levis with one branch of the wall, also protected by bastions and crenellations, which, proceeding west and cutting across the moats and the lower fortifi-cations, leads to the "way of the patrols,, (chemin de ronde) of the exter-nal wall of the Castle, thus joining the latter with the internal acropolis. At a lower point of this transverse branch of the wall, S t. A n t o n y's G a t e forms an exit from the Chora, i. e. from the lower part of the Castle lying outside of the "Castello,, or "Collachio,,. This gate will be included in the description of the walls.

Following the wall to the north of the Gate of Cannons, we come to another gateway, called by the Turks the "G u n p o s t  o f  t h e  O l i v e s,, (Zeitoun-tabie, plan I, 19), which used to be the entrance from the outside into the acropolis of the "Castello,,. South of the Gate of Cannons, the wall of this internal acropolis has been destroyed. But the present tower of the Clock stands now at almost the exact spot of the southwestern corner to-wer of this acropolis; the street that starts from the clock and proceeds east, almost parallel to the street of the Knights, indicates the course of the southern wall of the internal acropolis; of this wall only the southeastern

*D' Amboise's Gate.*

corner tower near the harbour, where the inner wall joined the outside wall of the Castle, has been preserved.

### b) The Chora

Outside the wall of the inner acropolis (Castello or Collachio) of the Knights, in the heart of the bazaar which is the starting point of the main streets going west or south, there is an important building of the Knights known as "Castellania,, (plan I, 20, formerly a mosque: Bezesten-dj.); this used to be very large and perhaps leaned against the wall of the harbour, but today only its southwestern part is in existence.

In the ground floor, a large gallery opens onto both façades, with two semicircular arches on the sourth side and a lower one on the west side. In the upper floor, on the southern façade above the lengthy carved belt, there are 2 rectangular windows and, higher, three stone gargoyles (identical with those of the Inn of France) and 3 stone "flagbearing,, rings. The west front is more sophisticated. An external staircase (an Aegean characteristic as we pointed out with regard to the Inn of Auvergne), leads up to a small terrace with a parapet and horse - block on the inside. Behind this, the upper-floor facade shows, above a belt, a window which is iden-

*Souleiman's mosque.*

tical with the others, and preserves its marble tracery with lilies in relief, as well as 3 flag-bearing rings near the roof. To the left of the window, an elegant Gothic frame — a flamboyant arch with twisted small columns — surrounds amidst plant decoration the coat of arms of the Great Magister D' Amboise and the date 1507. Further to the left and vertically to the terrace, there is the doorway leading to the upper floor, with an orna- mented rectangular Renaissance style frame: flames at the doorposts and various coats of arms (of the Order, of D'Amboise, Villiers De l'Isle - Adam, etc). around an angel on the lintel.

This large building is most probably the medieval Basilica Mercatorum, a centre where merchants met to conduct business in the ground-floor gallery, while the upper floor housed the headquarters of the market law court, i. e. the office of the "Bailli du Commerce,,, a Knight in charge of administering justice in trade disputes. A nice specimen of the architecture of the period around 1500, it is reminiscent of the Inn of France by some of its elements (windows, gargoyles, etc.) whereas the composition of the architectural elements —as well as some details, such as the marble door— clearly show the intermin- gling of late Gothic and Renaissance.

From the "Castellania,,, the noisy Bazaar street proceeds due west and terminates at a square, where the mosque " S o u l e i m a n - D z a m i,, (plan I, 21) stands in a triangular courtyard with plane-trees and a "basin,, for the purification of the faithful. It was built in 1808 in the place of an older mosque erected by the conqueror of Rhodes Souleiman II, which again was believed to have replaced a church dedicated to the Apostles. This is the last of the mosques built by the Turks. For the door, they used a lovely and characteristic Renaissance frame (resembling some Venitian frames), consisting of small columns decorated with sculptured garlands in front of door-posts with cherub-heads, hourglasses, armours and other war sym- bols; it was perhaps taken by the Turks from some tomb in a Christian church.

Across from the mosque, to the south, there is the noteworthy T u r- k i s h  A h m e t - H a f u z  l i b r a r y, founded in 1794 by this moslem Rhodian notable and containing many Turkish, Arabic and Persian manus- cripts (some illustrated), including an anonymous chronicle of the last siege of 1522.

On the road leading from the Souleiman mosque to the western wall, on the right and near St. George's tower, there is a peculiar Byzantine-Gothic Monastery known as " H o u r m a l i - M e d r e s s e ,, (School with the date tree, plan I, 22). Around the courtyard there is a number of cells (those on the north and the west side, on the ground floor, are old arch- roofed, with a door and a window. The elegant church whose entrance is now on the north side, has a four-conchaed design; before the altar, there are holes in the floor where the iconostasis was initially fastened, there are 4 three-lobed windows on the slender vault. Later, a porch was added on the north side and a narthex on the west side, both with Gothic pointed cross- vaults. The plan, the iconostasis, fragments of frescoes with Greek inscrip- tions fallen on the ground and found in 1922, indicate that this was a Greek orthodox church, perhaps St. Mark's, conceded in 1457 as a monastery to the Franciscans, who probably added the narthex and the west porch later; but also the Byzantine church itself shows traces of western influence (form of arches, ornamentation of vault, door-posts, etc.) and cannot be older than the 14th century.

Also the small mosque S a n d r i - T z e l e p̌ i (plan I, 23) situated between two medieval houses to the north, is a church in the shape of a free cross with unequal arms; the entrance is on the north arm, and the central square at the crossing of the arms is covered not by a vault but with a semicircular wagon arch. At the end of the street of Hourmali-Medresse, St. George's Gate opens on the wall (plan I, 24). During the early period of the fortification, prior to the siege of 1480, this gate led directly outside, but when the fortified enclosure was later enlarged, the gate became an internal one (now closed). The coats of arms of the Order and the Great Magister De Lastic used to be displayed above the gate, but they were partially cut away when the pointed arch was made later.

Back again at Ahmet Hafuz's library, the first side street to the right leads into the heart of the T u r k i s h   s e c t i o n, which has lost nothing of its medieval colour: its streets and lanes are still exactly as they were at the time of the Knights, and many of its houses preserve their original decorations on doors, windows and façades. The Turkish modifications lattice —windows, arch-roofed passages in the streets added to support the houses against earthquakes— have often enhanced the charm of the Turkish section by increasing its duskiness and enveloping the houses in an oriental, introverted way of life.

On the righthand side of this street, the courtyard of T a k e d z i-m o s q u e (plan I, 25) can be entered through a doorway with a double-sloping lintel and a semicircular concha above; this is also a church in the shape of a free cross (entrance from the north arm), wholy covered with pointed arches, and with a vault which is cylindrical on the inside dodecagonal on the outside. The church was built, perhaps, in the 15th century, and it has been suggested without assurance, that it may be the Saviour's church mentioned in the chronicles of the siege of 1522.

The first side-street to the left after this mosque, leads to a small square with a plane-tree, and a purification basin. Here we find S u l t a n   M u s-t a f a s'   m o s q u e (plan I, 26) built in 1765, and the Turkish "hamam,, formerly known to travellers as "S o u l e i m a n's   b a t h,,; this was probably built at the same time as the mosque and it is famous especially for its large square waiting-room which is covered with a vault and its floor is paved with ancient marble.

Not far from the Sultan-Mustafa mosque to the south, there is the A b d o u l - T z e l i l (o r   T s i o u k o u r)   m o s q u e, located lower than the street-level and reached by a descending flight of steps (plan I, 27) also a former church: the entrance (with a pointed concha above) gives access to the north side of the building, into a Gothic porch (pointed cross-vaults, a stone bench all around) from which one descends to the church, consisting of two aisles, each covered with a pointed arch. In the courtyard, to the east, there are cells indicating that this was a monastery — either Greek orthodox or Franciscan. The Gothic porch is of the early 15th century, the rest of the buiding is older.

At the southern end of the street, S t.   A t h a n a s e's   G a t e leads through the wall. This too, like St. George's Gate, became an internal one when the fortifications were enlarged. It seems that it was permanently closed with masonry by the Knights themselves for greater safety. According to Turkish popular tradition, it was through this gate that the conqueror Sultan - Souleiman entered the Castle and he had it permanently closed behind him to ensure that the town would remain in the hands of Islam. This is why the Turks used to call it "Pekeli Kapu,, = closed door. However, contrary to former belief, the Persian inscription on the south side of St. Mary's bulwark does not refer to this occurrence. Above the arch spanning this gateway is Del Carretto's coat of arms and the date 1515.

To the left of St. Athanase's Gate, and leaning with its south side against the inside of the wall is the small B a b - u - M e s t o u d  m o s q u e (the mosque of the built-up door, plan I, 28), a little church with a single aisle, a semicircular apse, a door with a semicircular concha and a small window on the front side (west), perhaps dedicated to the saint of the gate (St. Athanase) and dating from the early 16th century. In the same area, near the south wall and a little farther east, there is the small A l e m n a k  m o s q u e (mosque of the flag-bearer — plan I, 29 — founded by Souleiman's flag-bearer, according to the Turkish tradition): a small church with a single aisle, with a pointed arched roof, an apse which is semicircular on the inside and four-sided on the outside, a main entrance with a low arch and a semicircular concha above, on the north side; probably a Greek orthodox church of the early 15th century (on the east side there is a flag-bearing ring with a cross of orthodox shape).

In the centre again of the Turkish section (to the north), in a square with plane-trees and a fountain, is the R e t z e p - P a s h a  m o s q u e (plan I, 30), which was built in 1588 and is the most important of the Turkish buildings: the columns of the porch and of the fountain were taken from older churches—Byzantine or the Knights'; of the earlier richly ornamented exterior, there still remain a fair number of coloured Persian tile work ornaments with plant forms, identical with the so-called plates of Lindos; in the interior, verses from the Koran are written in enamel on the sides of the "Michrab,, (=prayer concha); in a vault-covered arch on the east side, there is the sarcophagus of Retzep-Pasha, the founder of the mosque.

Near this mosque, to the west, in the middle of a maze of arch covered lanes with many remains of medieval houses (one of the most picturesque parts of the Castle), there is the small Peial-el-din mosque (plan I, 31): it is an elegant little Byzantine church in the form of a free cross, the arms of which are covered with wagon arches; at the crossing, an elliptical vault; the apse is four-sided on the outside; the interior walls were covered with fine paintings, some of which have been preserved beneath the Turkish wall plaster.

Farther toward the centre and to the north, the D e m i r l i  m o s q u e (the "mosque with iron bars,, meaning the heavy railing of the windows which are flush with the street, plan I, 32) is a large and very important Byzantine church. Its form is a framed cross, i. e. a cross inscribed in a square, with three tripartite apses on the outside; the nave and the arms of the cross have a semicircular arched roof, but the aisles, which are lower, have a pointed arched roof; the vault is high on a circular drum with 4 windows; outside the west side door there is a Gothic porch with pointed ribbed cross-vaults (like those of Hourmali-Medresse). The form is similar to that of the Enteroum mosque, i. e. of the old metropolitan church we saw in the "Castello,,, and it has been suggested that when that was taken over by the Latins, the Greek Orthodox built this smaller church in its stead in the 14th century; the Gothic porch is a later addition.

At approximately the same level, farther east, in a little square near the bazaar, there is the Ibrahim-Pasha mosque (plan I, 33), built in 1531, and therefore the oldest of the Turkish religious buildings; however, as it has been repeatedly renovated and heavily plastered, no interesting architectural details can be seen. To the east of this mosque, a street proceeding south almost at right-angles leads to the K o s k i n o u Gate of the south wall; to the right, on a side lane near a low hill with a windmill on top is the small Houdai mosque (plan I, 34), a church of the period of the Knights: a single aisle, a pointed arched roof over the western half, the part toward the apse with pointed cross-vaults.

Nearby, the K o s k i n o u (the name is medieval), o r St. John's G a t e (plan I, 35) gives passage through the south wall. The inner part of this gate, too, is part of the older fortifications. Over the outside of the earlier gateway there are the coats of arms of the Order and of the Great Magister De Milly. To the right (when going out the door), there is a very important bilingual —Italian and Greek— inscription dating from the time of the same Great Magister (August 20, 1457), the Greek part of which reads: "T h i s w a l l o f R h o d e s w a s e r e c t e d a n d r e b u i l t e n t i r e l y, w i t h m e, M a n u e l K o u n t i s, a s o n e o f t h e m a s t e r m a s o n s,, proving considerable participation of local craftsmen in the great constructions of the Knights (though it is unknown whether only craftsmen and technicians or also architects were used).

The Italian part of the inscription, refers to this Kountis as "proto-maistor muradur,, = master wall-builder, and states that he was "proto-maistro de tuta la mura nova de Rodo,, (fig. on p. 77). This first gate is flanked on the right by a large rectangular tower, showing in a frame on its south side the coats of arms of the Order and of the Great Magister Fluvian under a picture of St. John. There follows a second gate displaying the coats of arms of the Order and of the Great Magister Zacosta. When the Great Magister D'Aubusson repaired and reinforced the walls, he added a strong polygona bulwark in front and another moat, and it was then that a third gate was made in the bulwark. This third gate is the most spectacular of all; in a richly ornamented multiple flamboyant frame over the low-arched opening, the coats of arms of the Order and of D'Aubusson are shown together with St. John's picture (pl. 46).

From Koskinou or St. John's Gate, a tortuous street running along the boundary between the Turkish and the Jewish sections leads to the D o - l a p l i - m o s q u e (plan I, 36), (dolap = well wheel) one of the most re-markable medieval churches, in the form of a free cross. In front of the north arm (including the entrance) a square space covered with an octag-onal pointed vault (perhaps a baptisterium) was added subsequently: the arms of the cross and the nave have a pointed arched - roof, the vault has four windows on the drum; the floor is covered with square marble stones interspersed with round red stones; before the altar there are holes in the floor for the iconostasis. The frescoes beneath the wall plaster seem

*The Inscription of Emmanuel Kountis on the walls.*

noteworthy. The doorway on the north side has a pointed concha above and on the right and left side shallow hollows in the shape of a latin cross filled with coloured slabs like the tileworks of Lindos. The main entrance with a pointed concha above and a finely worked Gothic frame supported by a carved horizontal belt is on the west side. The church probably dates from the middle years of the 15th century, and for all the Gothic details, the general plan and the iconostasis suggest that it was a Greek Orthodox church.

A little farther southeast, enclosed by a fence, is the little m o s q u e known as I l h  M i c h r a b (plan I, 37) (meaning: the first prayer concha), reputed to be the first Christian church in which the conqueror prayed to the Prophet upon entering the town. Its plan, irregular because of the surrounding buildings, includes three aisles and an apse; the nave and the south aisle have a pointed arched roof while the roof over the north aisle is semicircular; the interior walls are covered with frescoes of considerable importance, now mostly destroyed by humidity or overlaid with plaster; a few figures of saints are visible in the apse of the nave. The west side (with the entrance door) was plastered with coloured material. The building dates from the 14th or 15th century.

Proceeding through the J e w i s h section (which like the Turkish section, includes many remains of medieval houses), we find at its northeastern end, near the G a t e  o f  t h e  M i l l s, the poor ruins of the Gothic church of St. M a r y  o f  V i c t o r y (plan I, 38) built by the Great Magister D'Aubusson following a vow made to St. Mary during the siege of 1480, when she appeared to the besieged who were particularly hard-pressed at this point of the wall and brought them victory. The church was partially destroyed during the 1522 siege, and the only parts of its ruins still extant today are a few fragments of the apse and a few abutments from the aisles, all purely Gothic. Beside the ruins of this church, there is, in the wall, the so-called G a t e  o f  t h e  M i l l s (plan I, 39), one of the only two gates of the medieval harbour wall, then probably known as S t.  C a t h e r i n e' s  G a t e. It has a pointed arched opening, a protective balcony above and below the balcony, the coats of arms of the Order and, possibly, of D'Aubusson.

Turning to southwest, we meet the main street of the Jewish section, which runs almost parallel to the line of the harbour wall and terminates at the Bazaar and the "Castellania„, the old St. Catherine's hospital (plan I, 40) of the Tongue of Italy, built by the Italian Knight Fra Domenico d'Allemagna in 1392, and revonated by the admiral of the Tongue Constanzo Operti in 1516. Like the big hospital in the "Castello„, this too was both a hospital and a guest-house, though only for noble Italian travellers. On the ground-floor façade, there is in the court-yard the pointed arch of the entrance, and on the upper floor façade there are windows, and, in a frame, the coat of arms of Del Carretto, St. Catherine's wheel of martyrdom, and the coat of arms of C. Operti.

A little farther on the same side of the road, going through the door marked No. 2674, we find among houses, the remains of a Gothic Church, the largest of the Latins in Rhodes (30 m. × 18 m.), possibly the one referred to as "Sainte-Marie du Bourg„ (plan I, 41). Preserved are the three apses on the east side (three aisled), supported by posts with capitals decorated with plant forms, one of the posts separating the aisles and, on the south-western side, a concha with a pointed cross-vault (chapel).

The same street leading to the Bazaar and to the "Castellania„, forms a small square, which should be the medieval St. Sebastian's Square, if the small church now known as Engioli or Jeni-meszit (plan I, 42), a Latin single-aisle church with two cross-vaults is indeed the church dedicated to that saint.

On the north side, amongst other buildings, there is the façade of one of the most important urban buildings of the period of the Knights known by its old (but incorrect) name of "Palace of the Admiralty„ (plan I, 43). In the ground floor there are five store-rooms low-arched openings and off to right there is the entrance doorway in the courtyard, pointed and framed with carved bars and including a second pointed arch in relief; above this, a coat of arms with three banners and a dove on top. On the upper floor level there is a sculptured belt with a carved grid design running across the whole width of the façade; below the belt, at the exact centre of the building, there is a Latin inscription: "Pax huic domui et omnibus habitantibus in ea„, which is repeated in Greek in the courtyard. Touching the belt are the four large upper floor windows; they are rectangular, framed, identical with the windows of the Inn of France and of the "Castellania„ and between them there are other smaller windows. Smaller windows can also be seen higher up at different levels, and between them small rectangular frames used to include Greek inscriptions (one only: M P Θ Y, is legible at present). The middle of the roof over the central pair of large windows is higher than its parts on either side of this middle section. In the courtyard which is entered through the pointed door, there are store-rooms all around and a staircase with three flights (there is a well below the second flight) leading to the upper floor; at the wall facing the first landing there is a window and below it a coat of arms with three banners and the Greek version of the Latin inscription quoted earlier.

The staircase leads to an open passage giving access to a large hall in

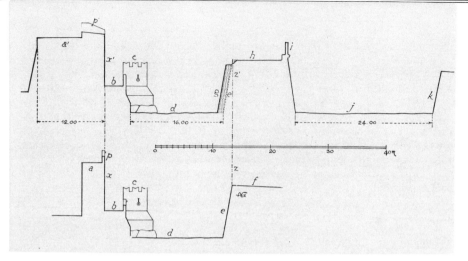

*Vertical section of the fortifications system (Gabriel).*

*Ground plan of the walls and the posts of the Tongues in 1522 (Gabriel).*

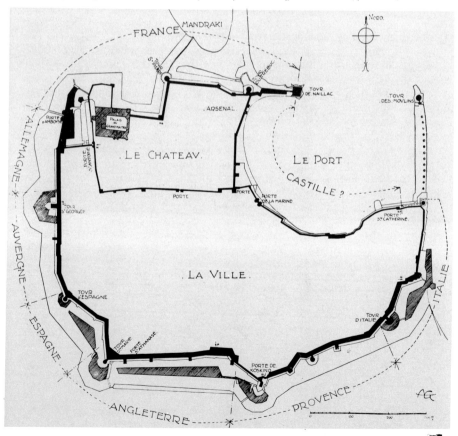

the middle of the front side (the two paired large windows of the façade belong to this room), in which the old hearth is preserved; all around there are other rooms including, at the northwestern corner, the kitchen with a fireplace, a small oven, and a well. "This is the most intact and most uniform example of a wealthy house of Rhodes in the 15th century,, (Gabriel). The religious symbols and the inscriptions suggest with near-certainty that this was the mansion of the Greek Orthodox Bishop of Rhodes. The style of the façade, the stressed centre and the regulation of all the other elements according to that centre (the off-centre entrance notwithstanding), the predominance of the horizontal, again show, as in a number of cases referred to before, the beginnings of the influence of the new Renaissance style mingled with the otherwise purely Gothic architectural forms.

## 2. The Castle Walls

### General aspects

The walls of the Castle of Rhodes are important in more ways than one. An integral whole so magnificently preserved is rare anywhere. Significant historical occurrences are associated with these walls, in particular the two famous sieges of 1480 and 1522, respectively. But the walls are instructive, in fact fascinating, for other reasons as well: for in their present form, they belong to the very period of transition, in which the discovery of the firegun brings about a radical change in warfare, reduces to uselesness the defenses of the medieval castles (so strikingly exemplified in this part of the world by the fall of Constantinople in 1453) and makes necessary a new kind of heavy fortifications; the Castle of Rhodes is in itself the narrative of the growing anxiety of the Knights as new experiences warned them over and again of their danger and it tells of their repeated efforts to adapt the old wall to the requirements of the times and to the new inventions in defensive warfare. The Castle of Rhodes was an object of admiration for its solidity to the people who lived and experienced the events of those dramatic years with the acute sensitivity of personal involvement — rather than with our own remote spectators' interest; travellers of the time described it as impregnable (inexpugnabile).

The West was keenly interested in the new outpost and bulwark of Christianity. In 1521, shortly before Souleiman's fatal siege, the Italian engineer Matteo Gioeni, who had played some role in the renovation of the fortifications, prepared a plan of the Castle of Rhodes in relief, and this was sent to Pope Leo X (the Medicis, the one with whom Luther quarrelled) by the Great Magister Del Carretto. One-and-a-half century later, Racine echoes the feelings of admiration and concern for the Castle of Rhodes in these verses:

"Rhodes, des Ottomans ce redoutable écueil,
de tous ses défenseurs devenu le cercueil,,          (Bajazet, 1672).

No less admired was the beauty of the Castle, and indeed its aesthetic value is considerable. Naturally, the Castle was first and foremost an engineering work born out of the moment's urgent and pressing needs; but there is no human work, no human expression, without a "form,, determined by the aesthetic criteria of its time. It is on this basis that an artistic examination and evaluation of the old fortifications of Europe is possible and relevant. The very top view of the walls, frequently reflects the predominant style of its period. (In Rhodes, for instance, the general contour and its parts are vaguely reminiscent of the type of four-concha shaped frame of sculptural and pictorial works so common in Gothic architecture). However, the Castle of Rhodes has not yet been studied from this point of view. Its artistic aspect and the style of the period are more evident in certain elements which, apart from their practical usefulness, had also a pronounced ornamental character, as e.g. in the gateways, or in the coats of arms decorating the walls; the oldest of these are shown in bas-relief in the Byzantine manner; there are others which are predominantly or entirely Frankish in character, and these must be studied to determine the exact interaction between the Greek and the western tradition. The change of style is evident even in inscriptions: the older ones down to the period of the Great Magister Zacosta (1461 - 67), are all in Gothic lettering, whereas from the time of D'Aubusson (1476), classical Roman characters, more fitting to the spirit of the changing times, are used.

The various stages of the efforts to improve the fortification are evident in the Castle itself; they can be dated, most of them fairly accurately, on the basis of some contemporary information, but mainly by means of the coats of arms of the Great Magisters who built or renovated the various structures. More than 150 coats of arms have been counted in various parts of the wall, from the oldest of H. De Villeneuve (1319-46) to the latest of Villiers De l'Isle-Adam (1521-23). The early Great Magisters do not seem to have done much more than just maintain and perfuctorily repair the existing Byzantine walls. Extended and methodical work was done only in the late 14th and in the 15th century (Hérédia, Naillac, Fluvian, Lastic, Milly, Orsini).

The new and really important works, however, were constructed under D'Aubusson, particularly after the 1480 siege, and completed by D'Amboise and Del Carretto. D'Aubusson was the most famous of the Great Magisters, and after his successful resistance to the siege by Mohamed II, he was made a cardinal by the Pope in 1489; he was altogether a very capable and energetic man, proficient in many languages, well versed in mathematics and especially in military engineering so that he was able to conceive and supervise the works personally; his coat of arms appears more than 50 times in various critical parts of the wall. In the last years, more particularly in the period of Carretto (1513 - 21), specialized Italian engineers are entrusted with the reinforcement of the fortifications. The craftsmen and master craftsmen were recruited locally, as mentioned in early sources and attested to by the inscription at the Koskinou Gate. How these craftsmen, who were rooted in the Byzantine technical and cultural tradition, were able to adjust to the new and essentially alien spirit is a challenging subject for investigation.

The various modifications carried out in the last 50 years of the rule of the Knights, aimed, to make the wall capable of withstanding gunfire as well as of striking at the enemy more effectively, by various adjustments and principally new exterior constructions, without spoiling considerably the old works, while the older towers are square, round towers become predominant in the 15th century. Experience had shown that the old, high and thin, walls were easily destroyed by gunfire, and that only large massive walls were capable of resistance. So they lowered the height of the wall and greatly increased the thickness on the inside especially in critical points, such as corners, gates, piers, covered the outside of tower bases with very thick low bulwarks, in order to bring their defense artillery as far forward as possible and increase its range; for the same purpose, they

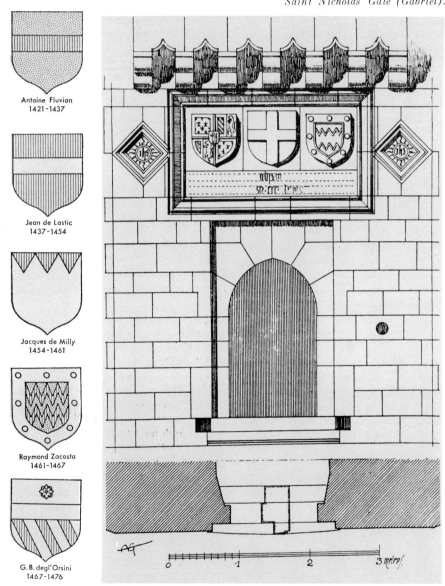

*Saint Nicholas' Gate (Gabriel).*

Antoine Fluvian
1421-1437

Jean de Lastic
1437-1454

Jacques de Milly
1454-1461

Raymond Zacosta
1461-1467

G. B. degl'Orsini
1467-1476

0    1    2    3 metres.

threw up strong oblong barbacanes (walls of earth) in the deep moat, their height reaching the level of the surrounding plain.

In the final form it assumed about 1500 with the combination of old and new elements, the fortification of Rhodes displays in most of its sections the following general plan from the inside outwards (see section on p. 79): 1) First, the inner w a l l (courtine) descends vertically down to the moat, or inclined to the moat base; on top of the wall runs the "p a t r o l   p a t h„ (chemin de ronde), protected against the outside by the p a r a p e t, which terminates with battlements and has various openings for large and small caliber weapons. 2) At several points of the fortifications, there is a second patrol path outside and at approximately half the height of the wall, called "f a u s s e - b r a i e „ (falsabraca); this again went as far down as the moat, and was protected by a parapet and occasional small towers; this ensured a lower line of fire covering the plain and the moat. 3) The m o a t, dug deeply into the rock, of varying width, the outward shore consisting of a high and strong "contre escarpe„, i.e. a solid wall to retain the surrounding loose earth. In Rhodes, the moat was never filled with water because it lies above sea level. 4) At a number of points, a second moat was added and between the two, high, thick, oblong "b a r b a c a n e s„ (ante murales) were erected, flanking the bulwarks or gates and merging with them, protected from the outside by a parapet and battlements.

The total fortified line surrounding the Castle of Rhodes was composed of: the land wall, the two ends of which came down to the two respective corners of Emborió, and there joined the harbour wall, and closed; and the fortified piers guarding the harbour, consisting of the P i e r   o f   t h e   M i l ls and of the smaller P i e r   o f   N a i l l a c, including the tower at the end of S t.   N i c h o l a s'   P i e r. Each of the eight ethnic groups or Tongues of the Order was responsible for one determined portion of the wall where it flew its particular banner together with the banner of the Order, thereby designating that particular portion of the wall as its own "post„ (post of France, of Germany, of Auvergne, etc.). During the last siege (1522) the posts of the various Tongues were as shown in fig. on p. 79 dawn.

Legend to fig. on p. 79 above showing section of the wall a = wall, b-c = fausse-braie and tower, d = moat, g = staircase to barbacane, h = barbacane, j = second moat, k = contre escarpe.


# Tour

Starting from the NW corner of the fortified wall, i.e. from the location of the Gate of Cannons and the Gate of D'Amboise, we see a complicate fortification system, the result of successive modifications and additions. An older transverse, high wall begins from the G a t e   o f   C a n n o n s (plan I, 18) and proceeding from east to west joins the inner wall of the "Castello„ or "Collachio„ with the outer fortifications line. Low in this transverse wall, S t.   A n t o n y' s   G a t e opened in a south-north direction and led out of the Chora (which lies lower than the "Castello„) and its wall; on the north side of this gate, over the semicircular arch, there is a poorly preserved representation of St. Antony in relief, and the coats of arms of the Order and of the Great Magister De Lastic. From this gateway, a long b a r b a c a n e proceeds in a northerly direction between two m o a t s; rectangular stone blocks from the ancient lower acropolis can be seen about halfway the inner (righthand) c o n t r e e s c a r p e. Reaching the north end of the barbacane, which is protected by a small polygonal bulwark, and turning to the right, we re-enter the "Castello" through the G a t e o f t h e G u n p o s t o f t h e O l i v e s (plan I, 19). If, on the other hand, we turn left at the bridge over the west moat before reaching the end of the barbacane, and follow the tortuous path, we come to the imposing D' A m b o i s e G a t e; when this was built, together with the new thick parts of the wall on its right and left, the older fortifications of the Gate of Cannons and St. Antony's Gate up to the Gunpost of the Olives, became entirely enclosed by the new fortified line. On the west (outer) side of the Gate of D'Amboise, over the semicircular arch and within a pointed frame, there are the coats of arms of the Order, and of the Great Magister with his name, and the date 1512; two solid towers flank the Gate right and left with their cylindrical volumes, with openings for guns on the roof. The bridge crossing over the new external wide moat is cut off shortly before the Gate, where the pont-levis used to be; its two perpendicular grooves can still be seen right and left over the entrance arch. This is one of the most beautiful gateways in the Castle: with the simplicity of its elements, using only the effects of the lines, the proportions and the sequence of its plastic masses, it conveys an aesthetic impression almost comparable to that of an ancient Greek monument. Here again one feels the influence of the new Renaissance trend, in sharp contrast to the purely Gothic effect of, say, the Gate of the Harbour (Marina). The p o s t o f G e r m a n y began at this point, extending to S t. G e o r g e' s t o w e r and its b u l w a r k. The wall has a f a u s s e-b r a i e on the outside.

St. George's stronghold is made up of an older square tower (the internal gate of the same name—see p. 73, plan I, 24—was described earlier) dating from 1421-31 and having on its west side a representation of St. George in relief, and the coats of arms of Pope Martin V, of the Order, and of the Great Magister Fluvian. The tower base was subsequently reinforced with a small four-sided, spur-like bulwark; in the time of the Great Magisters D'Aubusson and Villiers De l'Isle-Adam, the place was additionally fortified by a second larger and heavier bulwark around the earlier one (the coats of arms of these Great Magisters are shown on the north, northwestern and south external sides). At St. George's stronghold began the p o s t o f A u v e r g n e, which extended up to the T o w e r o f S p a i n. This portion of the wall includes a fausse-braie and a square tower, added in the years of De Lastic. With the repairs carried out by D'Aubusson, the wall in this area as well as in many others, reached a tremendous thickness of up to 12 m.

The T o w e r o f S p a i n, a round one, stands before the wall and exceeds its height by 3 m; its base is surrounded by a four-sided bulwark, showing D'Aubusson's coat of arms on the south side (D'Aubusson was a cardinal as well as a Great Magister by now) and the date 1489. The p o s t o f

S p a i n (Aragon) starts here, and extends to S t. M a r y 's  T o w e r. At this point, the wall has a fausse-braie with two rectangular turrets, and forms an inward angle. The coat of arms of the Great Magister De Lastic is displayrd both on the wall and on the parapet of the bastion. In the double moat, there is a barbacane which joins St. Mary's bulwark farther on. During the 1522 siege, the Turks succeeded in making a crack in this wall and a few days later the Castle surrendered.

S t. M a r y' s  T o w e r, also a round one, was built in 1441 by De Lastic, as shown by his coat of arms appearing below a relief of St. Mary on the external side of the tower. A wide moat separates the tower from its polygonal bulwark, which is flanked by a barbacane each on the east and the west side (on the south side of the bulwark can be seen the Persian inscription referred to earlier, see p. 73). From the eastern barbacane one proceeded to S t.  A t h a n a s e' s  G a t e (the gate permanently closed by Sultan Souleiman and described earlier), near a square tower (40 m. to the east of St. Mary's tower) showing on its south side Fluvian's coat of arms beneath a relief representation of St. Athanase with the Greek inscription AΘANAΣIOΣ, obviously a Byzantine building. St. Mary's tower and bulwark marked the beginning of the "p o s t  o f  E n g l a n d,, which extended to K o s k i n o u or S t.  J o h n' s  G a t e. In this part, the wall includes four square towers, a fausse-braie, an inner moat, a long barbacane, and an outer moat; the coats of arms of Fluvian and De Lastic on the wall determine the date of the construction. A little way to the west of the fourth tower, high up on the parapet and within a pointed carved frame there is a remarkable bas-relief showing St. Demetrios or St. Theodore down to the waist, with a lance and a sword. It has been suggested that the Saint is in fact a portrait of D'Aubusson whose coat of arms is also shown together with that of the Order.

The K o s k i n o u or S t.  J o h n' s  G a t e (described earlier, p. 76, plan I, 35, pl. 46) is fortified from inside to outside by: a rectangular tower dating from Fluvian's time (coat of arms on the south side) whose base is covered with a first four-sided, spur-like bulwark from Zacosta's period (coat of arms on the door), followed by a first moat, then a second polygonal bulwark, joining farther west the barbacane of the post of England and containing the external (third) Koskinou or St. John's Gate with D'Aubusson's coat of arms (the double carved belt decorating all around the top of the bulwark, with a pointed twist above the gate, forming a frame which encloses the coat of arms and St. John's figure as well as the gateway, is noteworthy); finally there is a second wide moat. This gate was the beginning of the post of Provence, which terminated at the round tower of Italy, also known as Carretto's tower. In this portion, the wall shows frequent outward and inward indentations, and includes a fausse-braie and three towers (the first of spur-like form, the second round with a polygonal bulwark at its base, the third square with a similarly shaped bulwark), and a moat whose width sometimes exceeds 40 m. Across from the first tower, the medieval contre escarpe of the moat cut through, and so exposed, a beautiful ancient conduit of an aqueduct or sewage system, built with skilfully hewn rectangular stones and covered with an arch, dating from the 2nd or 1st century B.C.

The round s t r o n g h o l d  o f  I t a l y (or of Del Carretto) an imposingly bulky work (50 m. diameter) is made up of an earlier inner round tower and, around its base, of a solid round bulwark, with 15 m. thick walls. The bulwark not only has opening for guns at the top, but includes in its main body an arch-roofed peripheral internal passage  reaching down to the level of the outer moat, and allowing through its low opening to open fire, horizontally on any invaders in the moat. The moat itself is accessible through this passage. The coat of arms of Del Carretto — who had this fortification made — appears repeatedly both on the bulwark and on the tower, with the dates 1515 - 1517. This is the starting point of the p o s t  o f  I t a l y, which extends to the G a t e  o f  t h e  M i l l s  or  S t.  C a t h e r i n e 's  G a t e. In this area, the wall forms first a number of angles, reaches the seaside, and at the foot of the Pier of the Mills turns inward into the harbour. It has a fausse-braie and a long barbacane which doubles the moat, and following the line of the wall in an irregular shape again reaches the sea and turns to the north. At the foot of the pier, there used to be a round tower with a polygonal bulwark at its base, now no longer extant.

S t.  C a t h e r i n e' s  G a t e, described earlier (plan I, 39) marks the beginning of the p o s t  o f  C a s t i g l i a, which ends at the small P i e r  o f  N a i l l a c at the foot of S t.  N i c h o l a s'  P i e r. To the west of the gate, the fausse-braie leads to a small three-sided bulwark. Thereafter, the wall runs along the shore of Emborió, includes an oblong tower bearing the coats of arms of Naillac and Orsini (the former built it and the latter repaired it), and reaches the famous G a t e  o f  t h e  H a r b o u r  o r  M a r i n a, frequently — but  incorrectly — referred  to as St. Catherine's Gate (plan I, 39, pl. 44). This is the most spectacular gate in the Castle, and was certainly more so when the sea came right up to it as shown in many old pictures. The opening in the wall is a semicircular arch; above this on the seaside a framed Gothic shrine contains in relief the figure of St. Mary between St. John (on the right) and St. Peter (on the left), the coats of arms of the Order, of France (3 lilies) and of the Great Magister D'Aubusson with the latter's now hardly legible founding inscription, dated 1478; in the corresponding position on the inside, there is a similar inscription and the representation of an angel in relief, with the coats of arms of the  Order and of D'Aubusson. The gate  is flanked on  both the inside and the outside by two oval rather than semicircular towers, whose base is not perpendicular but inclined, and the top of its back is underlined by a double carved belt; an identical second belt at a higher level, cuts in half the cylindrical body of the towers at the top, the crenellated roof is supported by a series of abutments crowning the whole with a highly ornamental interchange of lines and alternation of light and shade. The Gothic preference for slender forms, for marked vertical dimensions and (in its late phase) for picturesqueness is obvious here — so unlike the frugal plastic composition of the later Gate of D'Amboise (described earlier, see p. 83f). Thè interior of the towers, with three floors and various rooms, is well worth a visit.

A little farther north from the Gate of the Harbour, the wall turns inland at an angle, and finally joins the southeastern corner of the internal acropolis wall (the "Castello" or "Collachio"), thereafter proceeding north until it reaches S t.  P a u l' s  G a t e (it becomes a common wall for the Castello and the harbour). At the point of junction, a square door (with five coats of arms) gives access to a chapel with faded frescoes (older than the date 1456 written in coal). To the north, there are two square towers and, inbuilt in the wall: first a pointed frame with an angel in relief holding the coats of arms of the Order and of D'Aubusson, and a pertinent inscription dated 1478; follows a second frame, resembling a Gothic shrine, richly carved in a flamboyant style, similar to that of Castellania (previously described, see p. 72f), enclosing the coat of arms of D'Aubusson, now with a cardinal's hat, and the date 1494 (a similar example can be seen at the Inn of France, see p. 67). The remaining part of this wall included two square towers — demolished by the Turks in 1910 — with a 9.90 m. wide space between them. It is through this door that the arsenal of the Knights inside the wall communicated with the harbour. According to the ancient local tradition, the area of the arsenal was formerly (as early as the ancient Greek period) a small artificial inner harbour joined by the channel between the two towers with the external harbour of Emborió, and earthed up by the Knights in 1480. The same tradition has it that the famous Colossos stood over this con-

*The Gate of the Harbour (Marina) (Gabriel).*

· PORTE · DE · LA · MARINE ·

*The Pier of Naillac (Gabriel)*

necting channel and that the two, now dilapidated, towers right and left were the pedestals for its legs (in his imaginary reconstruction of 1826, Rottiers used this local popular belief as a basis — p. 43).

The small, fortified P i e r  o f  N a i l l a c (fig.on p. 88) and S t.  P a u l's G a t e are the starting point of the p o s t  o f  F r a n c e which extended all along the north wall of the Castle up to its northwestern end. From the harbour, the gate leads to a polygonal bulwark surrounding the base of a round tower (on the north side, a sculptured representation of St. Paul, and the coats of arms of the Order, of Pope Sixtus IV, and of the Great Magister D'Aubusson, indicating that the work dates from 1476-84); a door on the west side of the bulwark leads out of S t.  N i c h o l a s'  P i e r crossing the moat by a pont-levis first and a masonry bridge thereafter. From St. Paul's Gate the wall proceeds west toward the Palace of the Great Magister and, apart from the fausse-braie and the moat, it includes first two rectangular towers of the time of the Great Magister Hérédia, whose coat of arms appears on both; then, before reaching a round tower, in a graceful pointed, double - sloping frame a relief in which angels, a griffin, and a lion hold the coats of arms of the Order and of D'Aubusson (1477); then comes St. Peter's round tower with a sculptured representation of the saint with the coats of arms of the Order, of Pope Pius II Piccolomini and of the Great Magister Zacosta (1461 - 64) on the north side, and a polygonal bulwark around the base; at this tower, the wall turns sligthly due south, before it again turns west to join the east wall of the Palace of the Great Magister.The latter, strongly fortified with walls and towers forming a continuation of the outside wall overlooked and dominated all the surrounding countryside and the harbours.

The harbours had in addition their own fortifications. The smaller northern harbour of Mandraki, which was the military port of the ancients, and was referred to as "the galley harbour" by the medievals, was protected by the powerful s t r o n g h o l d  o f  S t.  N i c h o l a s at the end of the pier, which is 400 m. long, has three w i n d - m i l l s (pl. 31) of medieval origin (mentioned as early as 1496) standing on it and preserves on its east (external) side several pieces of the ancient pier. A medieval tradition had the Colossos standing at the end of this pier. The stronghold is composed of a very thick (17,30m. diameter) central round tower built by the Great Magister Zacosta in 1464- 67, showing on the east side a sculptured picture of St. Nicholas and the coats of arms of the Duke of Burgundy (who had contributed 10,000 gold crowns for this purpose), of the Order, and of Zacosta; the base of the tower is surrounded first by a moat and then by a strong polygonal bulwark, built by D'Aubusson after the siege of 1480.

The larger southern harbour (the great harbour of the ancients), referred to as "Port du Commerce" by the medievals and a port of vital importance for the medieval town, was protected on the land side by the Castle wall and fortified against dangers from the sea. East of St. Paul's Gate begins in a west to east direction the small pier closing the harbour on the north side; above this, a 12 m. thick wall built by Fluvian and D'Aubusson, joined a lovely older tower built at the end of the pier, by N a i l l a c (1396 - 1421); the tower was destroyed during the 1863 earthquake and only its base is extant today, but we know how it looked from older pictures. Upon this base which was made of ancient Greek materials, the square tower soared 46 m. above sea level; in the centre of the top, there was an octagonal turret, and surrounding this, four smaller round turrets stood at the four corners (p. 88). This tower, the work of Naillac, standing over the entrance of the harbour like an elegant lampstand, "panemnostos" as the medieval Greeks would have said, was a fine example of Gothic architecture by its involved slender form. A thick chain stretched from this tower across to the tower of the pier of the Mills blocked the harbour entrance for greater safety; the holes through which the chain passed, their edges worn with use, are still visible on the east side of the base. A length of thick chain kept at the military museum (St. Irene's church) in Constantinople is supposed to have been part of this chain.

Finally, a round tower with a circular bulwark around its base, also built on ancient Greek foundations, was erected about 1465 with money donated by the King of France Louis XI on the large pier extending in a south to north direction and closing the harhour on the east side, known in the Middle Ages as the P i e r   o f   t h e   M i l l s (there stood 15 mills, of which only three are extant today). Coats of arms  with the three lilies of France are displayed on the tower.

### 3. Outside the Castle

Within the Castle, where historical life was concentrated in the Middle Ages, almost all buildings are medieval, while hardly any traces are left of the ancient buildings. Outside the Castle, on the other hand, as a result of the same historical circumstances, the proportion is inverse: the ancient remains are both more numerous and more important, even though the tremendous building activity of the Knights left nothing but the foundations and occasional architectural members of the ancient buildings (fig. on p. 91).

In the northern area near the Governor's Residence and the building of the Port Authority, the small but remarkable m o s q u e   o f   M u r a t - R e ï s seems to have replaced St. Antony's Roman Catholic church, which was also a cemetery for common Knights. Its minaret is elegant. The Turkish cemetery, which on the contrary, was the one of the higher classes, contains the graves of many Turkish notables and alien exiles. The coffin of Mourat-Reïs, Souleiman II's admiral during the siege of Rhodes, lies in a circular mausoleum. There are many other fine graves including those of several Grand Vezirs and Pashas, of one Shah of Persia, of a poet named Mohamed-Ahmet-Efendi exiled by the Sultan because of his satires (1773 A.D.) and others.

In the Mourat-Reïs square, between the mosque and the Governor's Residence, fragments of the foundations of the ancient city's external wall which guarded the "small harbour" (Mandraki) on the land side, were found. Other ancient findings include 353 spherical stone missiles with inscriptions and markings indicating their weight, which ranges from 5 mna ($= 2.180$ gr.) to 10 talanta ($= 261.600$ gr.) (1 mna $= 0.436$ kg., 60 mna $= 1$ talanton). These missiles were intended for the defense of the wall: they were thrown or

## PLAN OF ANCIENT STREETS
### ANCIENT STREETS AND RELICS

| | | | |
|---|---|---|---|
| ▬▬▬ | Streets | ▬▬▬ | Walls |
| o ooo | Subterranean aqueducts | ▬▬▬ | Walls or terraces |
| o oo o | Aqueducts under the streets | ∨∨∨ | Harbour constructions |

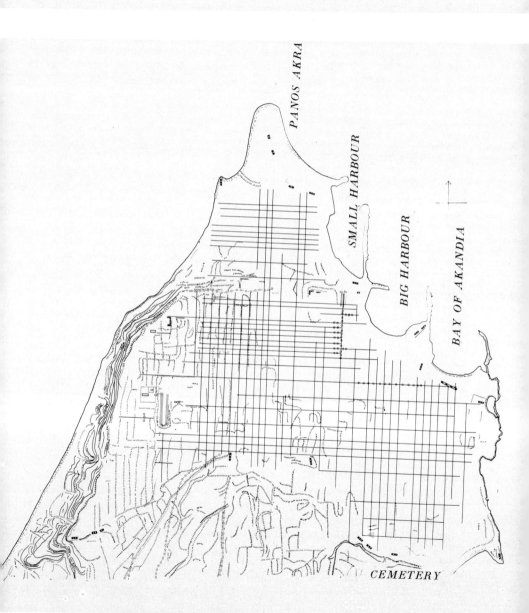

PANOS AKRA

SMALL HARBOUR

BIG HARBOUR

BAY OF AKANDIA

CEMETERY

rolled down upon besiegers; it would not be unreasonable to assume that they had been since the famous siege by Demetrios (305 - 4 B.C.) as the form of the letters on them would agree with that period.

A little farther west in the same area, at the east end of the quarter of Neochbri, a marble relief of St. Mary and Child (bearing at the back the coat of arms of Domenico d'Allemagna, founder of St. Catherine's hospital in 1392, above p. 77) is worshipped in the Franciscans' church to S t. M a r y o f V i c t o r y, built in 1743 and renovated in 1851; according to its inscription, the sculpture was discovered in the Jewish section in 1693 — which explains why it was called "Phaneromeni" (= the revealed one) and is believed by the Roman Catholics to have belonged to the old church of St. Mary of Victory, whose ruins we saw earlier within the Castle, at the southeastern corner of the wall (see p. 77).

Most roads in the valley to the west of the Castle between the Castle and the upper acropolis of St. Stephanos, follow the course of the ancient streets; such a one is e.g. the street called "M a k r y   S t e n o,,, starting from a crossroads south of St. George's tower, crossing the suburb of St. John, and then proceeding southwest with many ancient tombs on its left and right sides. No other ancient buildings have been discovered to date; based on a number of movable findings, it is assumed that in the Turkish cemetery near Tsimenlik's gardens was the ancient Asklepeion, while the Prytaneion was located behind the former Italian barracks Regina (see p. 58).

On St. Stephenos' hill — also known as Smith's hill from the name of an Englishman, an admiral brought here in 1802 by Napoleon's Egyptian campaign, i.e. on the u p p e r   a c r o p o l i s, ancient remains are much more numerous. The ruins of a temple dedicated to A t h e n e   P o l i a s and Z e u s   P o l i e u s can be seen on the plateau of the northernmost peak of the hill. The temple, with an east to west orientation, was of considerable size and, naturally, visible from the sea. Here the Rhodians kept the texts of all their treaties with other countries; in 163 B.C. to placate the Romans (see p. 20f) after they had suffered from their wrath in the previous years, the Rhodians erected in this sanctuary a colossal statue of the "city,, of Rome, which was 14 m. high. All this indicates that the sanctuary was one of the most highly revered.

A little lower than this peak to northeast, there is an interesting group of caves and channels connected with the underground water streams of the area; this must have been a "n y m p h a e o n,,, i.e. a sanctuary of the nymphs, whose worship was always associated with water springs. A large rectangular vestibule carved out of the rock is flanked on either side by an artificial cave with stalactite-like formations on the roof, and conchas-shaped niches or rectangular recesses carved out of the side walls, for statuettes and other sculptured votive offerings to the nymphs; from the middle of the long side of the vestibule, a subterranean passage descends to the deeper lying aqueduct. There is a number of such caves in the area. To the east of this region, there is a length of ancient road, which was paved in the Middle Ages; another part of this road becomes again visible farther south, on the slope of Sandourli.

Another interesting cluster of ancient buildings can be seen on the southern side of this peak. In a natural recess there is the S t a d i u m, which has been entirely reconstructed, but preserves only a few of its ancient tiers around the "sphendone,,, dating probably from the 2nd century B.C. Next to it to the north, in an almost square enclosure, is a small t h e a t r e; this too has been entirely reconstructed in its ancient form, based on the few remains found (pl. 47). It seats 800 and because it was situated in the vicinity of the stadium and the gymnasium, it has been postulated that it may have been used for the teaching of rhetorics by the famous orators of Rhodes. (The main theatre of the city, which was much larger, was probably located elsewhere on the hill or, according to some opinions, on the north side of the lower acropolis, in the area of the Arsenal Square and Dionysos' temple).

A short distance farther east from the stadium, a number of walls and several inscriptions were found, suggesting that here was the G y m n a - s i u m, the pride of the city and highly admired — like Dionysion down to the harbours — for its many works of art. Higher up and dominating all the other buildings was the sanctuary of A p o l l o P y t h i o s; the few remains found (foundations, columns, a triglyph, etc.) made it possible to reconstruct a corner of the temple (pl. 48). Remains of other related buildings including one which was probably a small temple of Artemis, have been found in the large precinct. As the group of these four important buildings — the stadium, the gymnasium, the theatre, and the sanctuary of Apollo Pythios — suggests, this region was one of the main cultural and artistic centres of ancient Rhodes.

Very near the stadium, to the west, there is a t o m b carved out of the rock, showing an architectural design. Other tombs were found further south on the higher part of the hill (altitude 111 m.) where some remains of the southern wall of the outer enclosure of the city have also been discovered. A large number of tombs were found on either side of the Makry Steno street : many of them are subterranean collective graves with square or semircular niches for the receptacles containing the bones or the ashes of the dead. To the south, this road joins the so-called s t r e e t o f t h e K n i g h t s, where ancient paving stones have been preserved; in the Middle Ages as in antiquity, this was the only road of communication between the capital and the northwestern parts of the island. Farther southwest, in the Sandourli ravine (which is the steep south apron of the acropolis hill), on the left of the street of the Knights, there is the so-called "d r a g o n ' s c a v e" in a location referred to by the medievals as Maupas or Malpasso (bad passage) Here, according to the legend, the Provençal Knight Dieudonné de Gozon, later a Great Magister (1346-1353), fought and killed a frightful monster that had been decimating men and animals.

To the south of the medieval Castle and of the suburbs of St. Anastasia and Metropolis, the road coming from St. John's Gate (Koskinou) crosses the ravine (Dermen-Dere) over an a n c i e n t b r i d g e: it is a wellbuilt, bridge with two semicircular arches and regular rectangular corner stones dating from the late Hellenistic or the Roman Period. On the left hand edge of the ravine, near and both right and left of the bridge, ruins of the outer

wall of the ancient city were found, including several remains of a s q u a r e
t o w e r which must have been there to protect some Gate. This is a very
important finding, indicating that the ancient enclosure extended to this point,
used the bed of the ravine as a support of the fortification and then proceeded (along an as yet unidentified course) to join the wall we have seen on
the southwestern peak of St. Stephanos' over Sandourli.

The walls and the ravine, the bridge and the road, the numerous (collective or
individual, chamber or subterranean) tombs to the south, all indicate that the area
has remained unchanged since antiquity. This assumption is reinforced by the presence
of the famous R o d i n i spring farther southwest in the same ravine. The coolness of
the water flowing in profusion, the greeness and the shade of the place would arouse
in the hearts of the ancients feelings of tender gratitude towards the benevolent mistresses of the waters, the Nymphs and their companions; they would probably have made
of this place a small open-air sanctuary, where they would pray, like Socrates : "oh dear
Pan, and all ye deities here present...,,. The old aqueduct crossing the ravine by a bridge
was probably built by the Knights and repaired by the Turks, but as it is entirely of the
Roman bridge-aqueduct type, it would seem that the subsequent construction was simply a renovation of an older work.

At a distance of approximately 10 minutes southwest of Rodini, amidst
various graves carved out of the rock, there is one that stands out because
of its architectural form. The people referred to it as " t h e   h o l l o w
r o c k,, in the last century but the Latin scholars of Rhodes named it, inac-
curately, "t o m b   o f   t h e   P t o l e m i e s,,—perhaps in remembrance of the
great temenos with the stoas erected by the Rhodians w i t h i n the city and
named "Ptolemaeon,, in honour of their friend Ptolemy and in gratitude for
his help during the siege by Demetrios. The rock has been hewn on the
outside in such a way as to assume the form of a large rectangular tomb
base, with a length of 27.80 m. and a height which probably exceeded 5 m.
All four sides form three steps leading up to the top surface of the base, the
edges of which are articulated and decorated each by a row of 21 non-fluted
half-columns, also hewn out of the rock, which would have terminated with
capitals (Doric since they have no separate bases). The east, south, and west
sides have been destroyed by waters and earthquakes, but the north side including the entrance to the tomb between the 5th and the 6th column near the
northwestern corner, has been well preserved. The doorway has two simple
stripes above, and gives access to a vestibule carved out of the rock, more
wide than deep, with a rectangular niche on each of the shorter sides. After
the vestibule comes the main chamber, which is narrower and deeper, and
is also equipped with large niches on all three sides — three on the right
side, five on the left, and two on the far side facing the entrance. The niches
were intended to receive the bodies of the dead or funeral urns. The surface
of all the walls was covered with a thin whitewash coat, still preserved at
places, and would have been coloured or even painted upon. It is not certain
at present whether over this hewn rock in antiquity there was a conical tomb
surface covered with earth and planted with trees, or whether the live rock
itself and additional carved stones were used to form a real small pyramid,

perhaps with steps — in which case the monument would have had the general shape of a mausoleum like that of Alikarnassos. This type of funeral monument, at any rate, is rather unusual on the Greek mainland, whereas it is fairly common in Asia Minor and its vicinity.

*Rhodian plates.*

# THE MUSEUM
# OF RHODES

The Museum of Rhodes owns a fair number of considerable sculptural works and a rich collection of small objects. We shall only refer in broad outline to the main categories of exhibits and we will describe only a few of the more important sculptural works[1].

The Museum includes findings; 1) from the Neolithic caves investigated in Kalymnos and Kos, such as clay pottery, tools (blades etc.), made from the shining black stone known as obsidian; 2) from the Mycenaean tombs of Ialyssos, such as vases, gold, ivory or moulded jewels, rings, scarabees, etc. 3) from the cemeteries of Ialyssos' historical period i.e. from the Geometric through the Classical Period, such as fine Rhodian, as well as Corinthian, and a few Laconic, vases, a number of black or red-figured Attic vases, figurines (terracotta) etc. A few clay sarcophagi, of the so-called Clazomenai type, beautifully ornamented with plant or human forms, date from the early 5th century B.C. and are among the last of their kind. The excavation of the sanctuary of Athene on the acropolis of Ialyssos also produced a large number of interesting findings; 4) from the more numerous graves of Kamiros, also rich in findings comparable to those of Ialyssos; 5) from the excavations of the sanctuary of Zeus Atabyrios, on the summit of mountain Atabyrion, mainly small bronze offerings, little oxen dedicated to the god, etc.

The Museum includes further: large clay jars with geometric decorations in high relief, often used in the Archaic Period as sarcophagi for children and young persons; Rhodian amphorae used for storage and transportation of liquids, with seals on their handles; inscriptions; architectural members; funeral monuments; christian mosaics; coats of arms of the Knights; tomb inscriptions of the Knights; ancient coins; coins and medals of the period of the Knights.

Sculptural works worthy of mention are: T w o  a r c h a i c  s t a t u e s  o f  y o u n g  m e n (kouroi) found in the acropolis of Kamiros in the area

---

1. (For a brief description of the contents of the Museum, as exposed today and written by the Ephor of Antiquities Rhodes Gr. Konstantinopoulos, in see p. 128).

of a later altar to Helios. They are good examples of the westernized Ionic forms of the Cyclades. The first, dating from the third quarter of the 6th century, is plain, and exhibits a tendency to exaggerated tallness and thinness; its general characteristics and its details (such as the backwards arranged hair) show it to be the work of a craftsman of Naxos. The second, dating from 530 to 520 B.C., was obviously made in Paros. There is more imagination in the typical design (outer contours, and internal contours of the abdomen, the thighs, the chest etc.); the rounded volume oscillates pleasantly between spherical and cubic forms, and a more organic sense of the body has resulted in successful plastic rendering of such parts as the hip joint, the thigh muscles, etc. (pl. 10).

The famous 2 m. high grave s t e l e o f C r i t o a n d T i m a r i s t a (pl. 17) from the necropolis of Kamiros. Two women, Timarista (the dead mother) on the right, and her daughter Crito on the left, embrace before parting forever. The daughter, a lighter and more subdued form, dressed in the thin sleeved Ionic chiton and wearing a himation, her hair cut short to indicate mourning, is turned to the side and caresses her mother's shoulder with her free right hand; the mother, a more dominant figure, a little taller than the daughter, her full body facing entirely front and the head only turned toward the younger woman, wears the Ionic chiton (with a sleeve on the left arm) with the heavier Attic peplos and a headdress. The two women, the living and the dead, are differentiated by their appearance and posture, in a simple way, discreetly implying that the dead woman is more important. The pyramidal form of the composition with the two similarly bent legs at the bottom, succeeds in suggesting that the two women are close and yet apart, the many perpendicular folds of the mother's dress from the waist down separating her from the living daughter, while the posture of her left arm and leg hint at a movement towards the right — out of the picture, and out of the world. Such suggestiveness achieved in so simple and yet meaningful a composition and by so restrained means of expression is an achievement of classical Attic art, as shaped by the creations of Phidias and nurtured by the spirit of ancient tragedy; were it not for Attic art, the Rhodian stele would have been inconceivable. And yet the stele is not an Attic but an Ionian work, as attested to by a rather more apparent sentimentality, by the excellent but softer relief work, and by the form of the upper part (round instead of horizontal or gabled as was customary in Attica); also, contrary to some opinions, it is not contemporary with Phidias but a little later dating from the last decade of the 5th century, as shown mainly by the inherent rhythm of the movement of the bodies, that is by a tendency to sharp bending.

Portrait-statue of a man, from Kos, 2.30 m. high. Dressed in a chiton and himation, the figure looks as if it were attempting to get out of itself. The posture of the body and the head does not follow a uniform line but is made up of a composite movement along several axes (legs, torso head), sharply cutting across one another in the three-dimensional space; the same is true of the lines of the folds. The young face bears a certain resemblance to Ptolemaean works, but this is not the portrait of a prince. It is a fine and instructive product of the latest phase of hellenistic baroque of about 150 B.C. (see p. 100).

Hellenistic portrait-statue of a young woman, from Kos,

*Roman mosaic from Cos, depicting a hunting scene (Rhodes, Palace of the G. Magister).*

1, 965 m. high. The posture is a slight modification of a type of statue that was common in the late 4th century B.C. and in the early Hellenistic Period; the representation of the dress, on the other hand, definitely belongs to the middle years of the Hellenistic Period. The contrast between the folds of the fine silk himation[1] and those of the thicker chiton, and the masterful way in which the latter are made to show through the former, is the precise style developed by the Rhodian sculptor Philiskos in his group of the Muses (described earlier), and of which this statue is a very instructive specimen; very fine face characteristics on an oblong egg-shaped head. The work dates from the second half of the 2nd century B.C.

Head of Helios, measuring 0.55 in hight together with the neck, with holes around the hair, where metal rays were fastened. It was found within the wall behind the Inn of Provence, not far from the top of the "Castello,, where the ancient sanctuary of Helios is supposed to have stood. The

---

1. The silk textiles of Kos, light and transparent, were famous in antiquity (vestes Coae). According to Aristotle, they were first woven "in Kos by Pamphile, daughter of Plateus".

*Muse Thaleia(?) out of a roman mosaic from Cos (Rhodes, Palace of the G. Magister)*

*Hellenistic portrait - statue of a young man (Castello, Rhodes).*

piece conveys the impression of a centrifugal force about to break out, an effect achieved by the turn of the head in relation to the neck (the effect would probably be accentuated by a similar turn in relation to the body) and by the broad waves of the rich hair. A very characteristic example of hellenistic baroque around the middle of the 2nd century B.C. (pl. 1).

Statuette of a nymph, headless, 0.63 m. high (pl. 26). The nymph is sitting on a rock and wears a himation which covers the lower and back part of the body, leaving the front part nude. This fresh small work of the early 1st century B.C. is not only instructive with regard to the momentary posture of the body and its relation to the design of the dress, which is a characteristic of hellenistic art, but is also important because, as mentioned earlier (p. 47), it copied closely the posture and dress of Dirce in the famous group by Apollonios and Tauriskos, is probably a product of the same workshop, and gives a much more true idea of the original than does the Roman copy of the "Bull of Farnese,, kept in Naples.

Statuette of Aphrodite, nude, 0.49 m. high (pl. 24), kneeling in the bath in an intricate posture, and spreading or wringing her hair. It is not an exact copy but an adaptation from a well-known Aphrodite by the Bithynian sculptor Doidalsas, dating from the early period of hellenistic baroque, around 200 B.C., and characterized by the intricate three-dimensional movement of the volumes of abundant flesh; the Rhodian adaptation, leaning more toward classicism, has greatly reduced the third dimension and the volume and, while preserving the general outline of the original, has turned the body forward, changed the position of the arms (in Doidalsas' work the hands are not busy with the hair but embrace the body) and has spread the composite motion over one plane, as in a relief. An elegant product of the 1st century B.C.

Statue of a woman, perhaps a nymph, stripped of her himation to her thighs, one foot on a high rock, the upper body bent and leaning on the raised upper leg. The apposition and contrast between the plastic curves of the body and the linear design of the garment, seems to have been the sculptor's main concern. For the rest, the composition and the attitude of the work, the previous remarks concerning the Rhodian adaptation of Doidalsas' Aphrodite, apply also to this nymph, which is of approximately the same age (pl. 25).

An interesting marble trophy measuring 1.90 m. in height, found in the necropolis of Rhodes (Makry Steno); it can be assumed to have stood over the subterranean grave of some Rhodian who had distinguished himself in the wars of Mithridates or Cassius, since it belongs to the 1st century B.C. It consists of a shapeless core (which would have been of wood), clad with a chiton, and wearing a breast plate and helmet, richly decorated with various designs: on the breast plate two griffins are tearing an "Arimaspos,, to pieces, higher up a lion is devouring a bull; on the helmet, two warriors are engaged in a duel, on the cheek-pieces there are gorgon representations. This statue is instructive both with regard to the hellenistic prototypes of the armoured statues of the Roman Period and with regard to the famous toreutic art of hellenistic Rhodes (see p. 45f) since it is obvious that this marble work must represent an imitation of the metal hammered breast plates and helmets actually used in the period.

# IALYSSOS
# AND KAMIROS

**1. Ialyssos** (pl. 50 - 52)

The location where Rhodes was built in 408 B.C. is part of "Ialyssia„, i.e. of the region of Ialyssos; it was on Ialyssos' coins that first appeared the symbol of a rose, subsequently adopted by the new city. Also, it is probable that of the three older towns, Ialyssos contributed the largest part of the new city's population, since in the years of Strabo, Ialyssos was a mere "village„. The old town lies some 10 km. west of Rhodes, farther inland from the bay of Trianta, on and round a 267 m. high trapeze-shaped mountain, known by the strange name Philerimos (or Philermos) since at least the 13th century A.D., but called Achaïa by the ancients.

The area is fertile and was inhabited from an early period. According to the legends, the first inhabitants were Phoenicians. The legends tell also of the ruse by which the Greek Iphiclos succeeded in driving them and their leader Phalanthos from Achaïa, where he was besieging them : an oracle had informed the Phoenicians that they would hold the land until ravens became white and fish appeared in wine jugs. Iphiclos, who had heard of the oracle, persuaded one of Phalanthos's servants to put fish in the water he fetched from the fountain, and Iphiclos himself caught some ravens and painted them white with plaster; the Phoenicians surrendered as soon as they saw these ominous signs. The priests of Poseidon in Ialyssos claimed that they were descended from the Phoenicians, and attributed the beginning of their cult to Cadmos, who had initiated it when he landed here after escaping the peril of a severe storm at sea. Certain elements in the cult of Ialyssos seem indeed to have a prehellenic origin, and a number of votive offerings found during excavations, may in fact point to a closer relationship with the Phoenicians.

The remembrance of the earliest Greek, pre-Dorian, colonization by the Mycenaean Achaeans, was kept alive in historical times by the name A c h a ï a of the acropolis of Ialyssos (on Mt. Philerimos), which must have been the first nucleus of colonization. After Rhodes was built, the only signification of the place was of a strategic nature, and it came to be known as the "S t r o n g h o l d„. Its harbour was called "S e h e- d i a„. Vestiges of the Mycenaean settlement were found around the village of Trianta, and a very great number of Mycenaean tombs have been discovered on the low hills of Moskou Vounara and Makria Vounara. In the Geometric, Archaic, and Classical Periods, Ialyssos spread over the north-

western slopes of Philerimos towards the village of Kremasto, and it is in the lower part of this region, around the little stream Daphni, that the rich tombs were found. Ialyssos was the home of the great family of the Eratides, of which the Diagoras, immortalized by Pindar, was a member. The poet Timokreon was also a native of Ialyssos.

The ancient acropolis of Mt. Philerimos (Achaïa) was used for military purposes by both the Byzantines and the Knights : here the Genoans besieged the Byzantines under Ioannis Kantakouzenos in 1248, and this was the first stronghold occupied by the Knights when they came to settle down on the island in 1306; here, too, Souleiman established his headquarters for the great siege of 1522. The intensive building activity developed in the Middle Ages led to the elimination of all but a few remains of the important buildings of the ancient acropolis.

The southeast triangular corner of the acropolis was reinforced with separate fortifications by the Byzantines and the Knights, so that it became a castle in itself with its own tower. On the opposite northwestern corner, two Byzantine lookout towers are still standing. The ruins of S t. M a r y' s m o n - a s t e r y and church built by the Knights in the place of an older Byzantine church, can be seen at the highest point of the plateau. At the back of a vestibule, there are two chapels separated by a wall; the one on the north side has cross-vaults and a pointed window, and on the abutments of the arches, are shown the coats of arms of the Order and of D'Aubusson. The chapel on the south side has similar cross-vaults, two pointed and two semicircular windows, and a small pointed shrine with a concha on the wall, where they would keep St. Mary's picture. Near the building of the Knights there are the remains of a small Byzantine church and beneath that, a small underground Byzantine chapel-shrine, whose walls were subsequently (14th-15th century) ornamented with frescoes by the Knights.

These medieval constructions were erected partly upon the ruins of a l a r g e a n c i e n t t e m p l e of the 3rd or 2nd century B.C., shown by inscriptions to have been dedicated to A t h e n e P o l i a s and Z e u s P o l i e u s. The style of the temple was Doric amphiprostyle tetrastyle, i.e. it had four columns each on the pronaos and opisthodomos (the same as the temple of Athene in Lindos, but larger). Inside the cella, in front of the western wall and along the walls of the long sides can be seen the foundations of an inner colonnade with smaller columns, and the rectangular base of the statue of the goddess. In front of this base and beneath it, there are the remains of the paved floor of an older temple. Various circular or irregularly shaped recesses in the walls, especially on the west side, served as "receptacles„ for offerings or for ritual purposes (pl. 52).

Preserving its character and charm to a much greater extent is a m o n-u m e n t a l  f o u n t a i n situated some 30 meters below the south side of the acropolis. In front of it, there is a small square with an enclosure, at the end of a few descending steps. At the rear, the rock has been slightly scooped out to receive the back wall of the fountain, which is nicely built, in the isodomic way and has four marble lion heads. The water reached the back wall of the fountain through a conduit dug out of the rock and flowed through two of the lion heads (the other two were merely ornamental) into a basin at the front. The front of this basin was closed by a "parapet„ consisting of slabs between six posts, with seven lion heads. On one of the posts, a now illegible inscription was a "sacred law„ concerning the use of the fountain. From the basin, the water flowed through 3 of the lion heads (the other four are ornamental) onto the floor of the porch which constitutes the façade of the fountain and has six Doric columns corresponding to the six inside posts. The fountain was roofed. This fine work dates from the 4th century B.C. (pl. 50).

*View of Kamiros.*

*Reconstruction of the temple of Apollo Erethimios (after H. Balducci).*

Noteworthy for their particular character among the cults practised in Ialyssos were : 1) the cult of A l e c t r o n a, a goddess connected with the Sun, probably brought over from Argolis by the Achaeans and identified with some local prehellenic deity; her sanctuary was situated at the east foot of Philerimos, but the exact location is not known; and 2) the cult of A p o l l o  E r e t h i m i o s, who was perhaps also a prehellenic deity, a patron of agriculture and more particularly its protector against the mildew disease. His sanctuary, a small Doric temple in-antis, of the 5th-4th century B.C., and a small theatre were found near the village of Theologos (Tholoo).

## 2. Kamiros (pl. 49)

Kamiros, the second of the three largest old towns of the island (pl. 49), is situated south of Ialyssos, on the northwestern seashore, not far from the village Calabarda and near St. Minas' cape (the ancient Mylantion). Its region, known as K a m i r i s, was smaller but more fertile than the areas of the two other towns; there were good fields, and many olive and fig trees. The symbol used by the town of Kamiros on the coins it had begun to mint as early as the 6th century B.C. was a fig leaf. As a result of the natural lay of the land, separated from the regions of the other towns by Mt. Atabyrion and its hills, Kamiros faces to Crete and the Peloponnese, and it is with these two areas that her earliest historical relationships were developed. The name Kamiros occurs in Crete as well (Hierapytna); the ancient harbour of the area, near Lagonia south of Kamiros, was called C r e t i n i a and here, according to the legend, the hero of Kamiris Althaimenes, son of the king of Crete Catreus, son of Minos, first landed on the island.

Althaimenes was induced to leave his homeland by an oracle which predicted that Catreus was going to be killed by one of his children. Upon his arrival, he climbed on

Mt. Atabyrion and scanning the horizon, he sighted Crete (they say that Dicte on Crete at a distance of 240 km., and, when the weather is good, even Ida, can indeed be seen from the top of Atabyrion); he was then reminded of his ancestral gods, and he erected an altar to Zeus Atabyrios. In the meantine Catreus, now an old man and wishing to hand over the kingdom of Crete to his son, came to Rhodes to find him. Althaimenes mistook him for a sea-robber and killed him; when he realized what he had done, he prayed for the earth to swallow him up, and this was his end.

The manner of death of Althaimenes as well as the cult of the "Mylantian,, gods in Kamiros (their names were Zeus Mylantios and Himalia, and cape Mylantion was named after them; they had taught men how to grind the corn and knead the dough) are expressions of the terrestrial element prevailing in all prehistoric religions. In the Historical Period, however, the prevalent cult in Kamiros was that of Athene Kamiras. From the rich cemeteries it can be inferred that, like Ialyssos, Kamiros was a flourishing city in prehistoric times, in the period of the Mycenean Achaeans, prior to colonization by the Dorians. It continues to flourish under the Dorians and well into the 5th century according, again, to the testimony of the graves. Peisandros, the poet of "Herakleia,,, was born here in the 7th century. Even after Rhodes was built in 408 B.C., Kamiros was not entirely deserted; ruins and inscriptions show that it continued to be alive and active.

The hill of the acropolis is sickle-shaped, with a NE to SW orientation. Its E, S, and W sides are steep, but in the centre is a small valley which slopes more gently toward NW, down to Mylantion. The residential section of the town spread down the sides of the valley, while religious and public buildings were situated on the higher southern part of the hill, where it forms a triangular plateau. The whole north side of this triangle, in a NE to SW direction, is taken up by a long Porch-like building, to which we shall return presently. At the rear of this construction, to the south, the first parallel walls belong, perhaps, to the enclosure of the s a n c t u-a r y  o f  A t h e n e  K a m i r a s. Another two parallel walls joined by a shorter transverse wall farther south must also be parts of the same temple, which seems to have been a peripteral, probably a hellenistic enlargement of the original archaic structure. In the floor and around the temple there are several deep circular and rectangular holes cut out of the rock; these were presumably "receptacles,, for offerings, but may also have been used for ritual practices.

Approximately 20 m. to the north, within the main body of the porch mentioned above, there is a large o l d e r  b a s i n, 17,40 m. by 10,20 m. and 3.20 m. deep. Its walls are plastered with a waterproof coat. Two flights of steps at the two opposite corners of the north wall descended to bottom, where two large circular holes served for cleaning the basin and were closed by two conical stone stoppers; but the wall built with regular stones which separates the steps from the holes is of a later date and belongs to the porch above. The basin dates probably from the 6th or 5th century B.C. and it has been estimated that it could hold 600 m³ of water, a sufficient quantity to meet the requirements of 300 - 400 families during the six dry months.

The basin was put out of use and filled up with earth in the Hellenistic Period, when the over 200 m. long porch, atready mentioned was built above, seemingly as a part of the market place. There were two rows of columns standing upon the first two long parallel north walls; the third, southern, wall is the front of a series of small rooms — living quarters or shops — opening on the second, i.e. the inner, colonnade; from their door-ways, three marble threshholds have been preserved in situ. An extended, carefully designed network of clay pipes and conduits fitted with valves, in association with various wells and subterranean reservoirs, was now used for the collection and distribution of water; as shown also by similar works in the residential section of the town, the water supply was a matter attended to very carefully in Kamiros. According to the few architectural members preserved, the porch was of the Doric order and built in the 3rd century B.C.

Three-and-a-half metres north of the front wall of the porch, before the archaic basin, there is the foundation of a small h e l l e n i s t i c  t e m-p l e  o r  a l t a r, measuring 2.32 by 2.24 m., with three steps on the west side.

Farther north, in the lower parts of the valley sides, many houses of the Hellenistic Period, resembling the houses of Delos and Pergamon, have been found. Geometrical decorations in colour or sculptured imitations of architectural members can still be seen on several walls. Also in this area, a n o t h e r  s a n c t u a r y centered around a Doric temple in-antis of the 3rd century B.C. has been discovered. It included altars dedicated to various deities, as well as statues and inscriptions in honour of various persons.

Nearly all of the hills surrounding the ancient town — Makry Lagoni (the stele of Crito and Timarista was found here), Kechraki, Pateles, Kasbiri, Papa-Loures, Fikel-loura, etc. — are full of innumerable graves containing a multitude of funeral offerings. These are perhaps the most extensive cemeteries in the whole of the Greek world.

*Kamiros. Restaured peristyle of a private house.*

# LINDOS

*Here, the wise Rhodian, Cleoboulos, sleeps,*
*And over his ashes sea-proud Lindus weeps.*
*(Diogenes Laertios)*

### General Remarks (pl. 55 - 64)

Lindos is in fact the rock of Lindos. It is the rock that dominates the area of Lindos a little lower than half-way down the east coast of the island as it juts out of the sea to a height of 116 m., forming a smaller and a larger port to its right and left (north and south). On and around its top, Lindos "proudly delights in the open sea,, (quoted from a hellenistic epigram), open wide to the south (pl. 55).

A number of findings suggest that Lindos was, or had been, inhabited in the Neolithic Age (2500 - 2000 B.C.). From the scarcity of Mycenaean findings (from 1500 B.C. onwards) it appears that in the period of the installation of the Achaeans in the island, Lindos was a settlement of secondary importance compared to Kamiros and Ialyssos. Lindos, however, caught up with and outran these towns in the Geometric Period after the Dorian conquest (10th century B.C. onwards). From the earliest of these Dorian centuries, the sanctuary of the ancient goddess worshiped on the rock of Lindos assumes an ever increasing significance. The Lindians become rapidly a seafaring people, and as early as 690 B.C., Lindos throws out colonies to Sicily and South Asia Minor; there also exists evidence of active trade exchanges with Cyprus, Phoenicia, and Egypt.

A prominent personality of Lindos in the first part of the 6th century B.C. was Kleoboulos, son of Evagoras and a Herakleid (i.e. of ancient royal blood), a contemporary of Solon and Peisistratos; he governed his city for 40 years, fought against the Lycians of Asia Minor, improved considerably the sanctuary of his city, and became known all over Greece as one of the seven wise men, for his moderation and his democratic government. Following the Merger (Synoecism) of 408 B.C., which deprived the three older cities of any individual political life, Lindos maintained its importance to a far greater extent than the two others, due to the old sanctuary of the Lindian Athene which had become, and remained for a long time thereafter, the principal religious centre of Rhodes, and famous throughout the eastern Mediterranean.

Information or monuments from the Byzantine Period of Lindos are scarce. We will only recall the 10th century scholar Constantinos who concerned himself with the

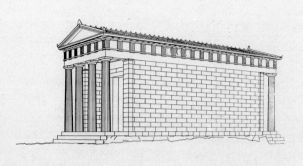

ancient epigrams of the rock (see p. 52). The Knights renovated and reinforced the Byzantine castle; when they rose against the first Great Magister Foulques De Villaret and deposed him in 1317 A.D., he came here and shut himself off with his own people until he left for Avignon. The castle of Lindos, too, surrendered to Souleiman in 1522. From subsequent periods, especially from the 17th century, there are in Lindos some architecturally very interesting buildings, in which experts see a strange intermingling of old local, Byzantine or oriental elements with western influences introduced by the Knights. We would repeat in this connection the suggestion repeatedly made above, that these cross-influences should be studied not only from the negative point of view, i.e. not as an inorganic mixture of discordant ingredients, but also as a positive fact, as the expression of a new and composite sensibility.

Under these circumstances, what may most interest the visitor, apart from the effect of the scenery which is as striking today as it was in the past, is the S a n c t u a r y   o f   t h e   L i n d i a n   A t h e n e and its monuments on the acropolis (fig. on p. 110). The cult on the rock was extremely ancient. As the legend went, Danaos and his daughters stopped here on their way from Egypt to Argolis and erected the sanctuary and the statue in 1510 B.C. In his hymn, Pindar too, refers to the sanctuary as being prior to the Dorian colonization under Tlepolemos, since he describes it as being built by the immediate descendants of Helios. All this goes to show that prior to the arrival of the Greeks, a prehellenic goddess had been worshipped on the rock since time immemorial; her name is not known, but as she was closely associated with the rock, the rock's own was perhaps the only name she had : L i n d i a n (so in other places : Dindymene, Dictynna, etc.). It is characteristic that the Greeks, later, never referred to this goddess as just A t h e n e, but always as L i n d i a n   A t h e n e. She must have been a goddess corresponding to the matriarchal deities of the Middle Eastern religions, who were the mistresses of fauna and flora, protectors of fertility in man and nature, and were usually worshipped in high places. The prehellenic character of the goddess left its mark on her cult, long after she had become a Greek goddess, the Lindian Athene : at first there was no temple, and the worship was conducted in the "a c r o p o l i s   g r o v e,, (Pindar), which was carefully tended even after the temple was built. The first "image,, of the goddess set up by Danaos was "according to ancient

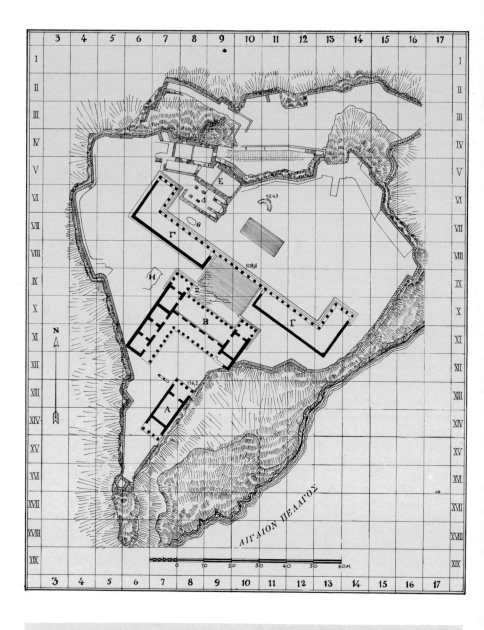

| | |
|---|---|
| **A** TEMPLE OF ATHENE | **E** ADMINISTRATION BUILDING |
| **B** PROPYLAEUM | **Z** ANCIENT STAIRCASE |
| **Γ** LARGE STOA | **H** BIG DEPOSIT |
| **Δ** MEDIEVAL CHURCH | **Θ** SMALL DEPOSIT |

practice,,, a rough plank (Kallimachos). What is more important, the goddess had no altar and no oxen (which had to be burnt subsequently according to the prevailing custom in other Greek sanctuaries of Athene) were sacrificed to her; the people only offered her fruits, sweetmeats, and drinks — "fireless sacrificial offerings,, in the expression of Pindar, who goes on to explain this peculiarity of the Lindian cult by saying that in their hurry to be the first to honour the newborn goddess, the Heliads had forgotten to take fire with them before they climbed the rock. The Dorians, and perhaps the Achaeans before them, identified the goddess with their own Athene, though the latter's war-like nature never became prevalent in Rhodes. During the Geometric Period, a temple was erected to the goddess; it was then that a first statue — a small wooden one — was made which showed the goddess seated in a throne with a crown on her head and garlands suspended from her garment's clasps. But never was an altar built or oxen slaughtered on the acropolis to the end of the ancient culture.

Around the middle of the 6th century B.C., Kleoboulos renovated the sanctuary of Athene; he built a larger t e m p l e on the top of the rock, probably of a plan not different from that of the present, subsequent buildings, i.e. amphiprostyle tetrastyle, adorned it with eight shields from the loot of his victories (one on each column i.e. four on each of the short sides) and ornamented the statue with a gold crown. Fragments of this archaic temple may still be extant within the later building, but they are indistinguishable. An a r c h a i c  s t a i r c a s e which can be seen under the n e w e r one, must also have been built by Kleoboulos. Shortly after the "Synoecism,,, perhaps in 407 B.C., the Lindians adapted their temple, according to the new classical taste, making it appear more monumental, by the addition of large p r o p y l a e a (fig. on p. 110, B), comparable to those of the Acropolis of Athens and of a n e w staircase over the archaic one. So the area of the temple was separated from the rest of the acropolis, like a separate s a n c t u a r y, the propylaea now making immediately evident the religious character of the building, and its aloofness from everyday affairs.

About 342 B.C., a fire burnt down the archaic temple of Kleoboulos together with the ceremonial statue and most of the votive offerings; promptly, the Lindians built a new one in its place, Doric amphiprostyle tetrastyle and made a new statue to the goddess; the new statue was bigger and was probably constructed by the new technique of "acroliths,, — which was cheaper than the chryselephantine — i.e. the body was made of gold-plated wood, whereas the limbs (arms, legs) and the head were made of marble or ivory; to ensure its stability, props fastened the statue to the wall; the goddess was now upright, holding a phiale in her lowered right hand, while her left hand rested on the shield (an echo of Phidias' statue of Athene), and again she wore a crown and garlands.

The reputation of the temple soon attracted new offerings, for it was, as the Chronicle of Lindos says : "most old and venerable and had been adorned since the oldest times with many and beautiful offerings because of the miracles of the goddess." This 99 B.C. inscription of the local scholar Timachidas, though a beginner's work, is important as it mentions several such old offerings, some of which still existed in his day, while others lived in the memory of the people or were described in older writings. In addition to prominent historical personalities, the donors included several mythical heroes; in the latter case, the offerings were mostly real and only their association with the mythical donors was imaginary; the ancients' implicit belief in the truth of myths is expressed by the relevant inscriptions. Out of the many mythical offerings (by the Telchines, by Kadmos, Minos, Herakles, Tlepolemos, etc.) the one reputed to have been offered by Helen of Troy deserves mention for its peculiarity : the gift according to the Chronicle was a pair of bracelets; other legends, however, reported the offering to have been a vase made of electron (gold and silver) in the form of a breast (breast-shaped clay offerings have indeed been found), made to the measure of her own breast, because it was the sight of that breast that had saved her from Menelaos' revenge in Troy. From historical times, the inscription mentions offerings by Kleoboulos, Phalaris, Amasis, Artaphernes, Alexander the Great, Ptolemy I, Pyrrhos, Hiero, Philip V, etc., and concludes with an enumeration of the goddess's miraculous acts.

But regardless of the information supplied by the Chronicle and other authors, the very remains of the monuments on the acropolis are impressive enough. In the Hellenistic Period, the limited space must have looked like a forest of bronze statues and other offerings. Today, only their p e d e s t a l s and inscriptions are in existence; even so, the historical, political, and cultural events we read about in books, suddenly begin to throb with life when they appear in these inscriptions. Take for instance, the statue base in the form of a ship's bow (near the east corner of the stoa marked Γ in fig. on p. 110) whose inscription tells of the wars of the Rhodians with the sea-robbers in 260 B.C. ; or the inscriptions telling of the wars with Philip V, or Antiochos, in the years 200 - 190 B.C., and mentioning the name of the famous admiral Eudamos; or that other inscription about Kallixenos, son of Megakles, author of "On Alexandria„ and artist (see p. 34), and a priest of Athene as well in the year 210 B.C. ; or that about the great stoic philosopher Panaetios, who was hierothytes at about 149 B.C. or the ones mentioning the names of artists, such as Lysippos, Pythokritos son of Timocharis who may be the master of the "Nike of Samothrace„, of Boethos from Chalcedon, of Athenodoros and Agesandros, the sculptors of "Laokoon„, etc. As mentioned earlier, the sanctuary included in addition a number of famous paintings.

In the Hellenistic Period, one of the most glorious in the history of Rhodes, the sanctuary assumed its final form by the addition of a l a r g e s t o a to its north side, i.e. at the entrance of the acropolis, around 200 B.C. (fig. on p. 110, Γ). Appearing by its shape to embrace the entering pilgrims, it occupies nearly the entire width of the entrance side and is situated in front of, and lower than, the two other main buildings (the p r o p y l a e u m to the N. and the t e m p l e to the E) which project stepwise behind it, the one higher than the other, and expresses the hellenistic fondness of spaciousness and deep perspectives. Peculiar, and characteristic of the religious spirit of the Roman Period, and its tendency to artificially revive old beliefs, is the s m a l l t e m p l e to the divinatory demon P s i t h y r o s (also worshipped in Athens as an attendant to Aphrodite, Eros, and Hermes) erected by one Seleukos near the north corner of the temple of Athene about the year 200 A.D.; there are a few remains of its Ionic or Corinthian columns and its stylobate; the bombastic epigram which has been preserved, however, mentions a "temple with many columns,, and of "excellent,, appearance, and goes on to affirm that Psithyros will not be satisfied with offerings of less than one drachme; the whole is strongly reminiscent of some fine poems of Kavafis. As late as the 3rd or 4th century A.D. the priest of Athene, Aglochartos, endeavours, as others had done before him, to preserve the old sacred grove that covered the space not occupied by buildings, and, as he informs us by the many epigrams he engraved in many parts of the acropolis, he planted "indestructible olive trees,, over and over again.

## The monuments outside of the acropolis

The church of S t. M a r y o f L i n d o s was built by the Great Magister D'Aubusson in 1489 - 90. It is cross-shaped, with an octagonal dome, a front porch covered by a cross-vault and above it the remains of a steeple displaying the coats of arms of the Order and of D'Aubusson. In the interior, the walls are covered entirely with frescoes, painted by Gregoris from Symi in 1779 (as stated by the inscription over the door on the northern side), and repaired in 1927. The carved iconostasis is worthy of note. There are additional frescoes (Virgin with Child, Saints), dating from 1675, outside the door on the north side.

Many of the old — 17th century — h o u s e s o f t h e v i l l a g e are extremely interesting, "built of regularly hewn lovely local stone, with medieval doors and windows adorned with ornamental motifs some of which are inspired by the art of the Knights, others by the Turkish art or the ecclesiastical Byzantine tradition,, (Maiuri). Such remarkable houses are those of Priest Constantin (1626), Moschoridis (1642), Makris, Makroulitsas, a.o. "Plates of Lindos,, and local woven articles can be seen in many houses (pl. 57).

West of the village, at a place called C a m b a n a (on the side of Mt. Krana), there is a monumental h e l l e n i s t i c t o m b, now ruined but known from drawings of the last century; its façade was similar to that of this type of monument in the city of Rhodes, it belonged to one of the most prominent families of Lindos, the family of Archocrates son of Archipolis as we are informed from inscriptions on funeral altars found there and was made in the early 2nd century B.C.

On the west slope of the acropolis, the ancient t h e a t r e was carved out of the rock; the "koilon,, (27 rows of seats) has been preserved as well as the orchestra circle and the position of the thymele but nothing of the stage itself. The foundations of some large ancient walls which formed part of the gymnasium of the ancient city exist near the theatre and around the little church of St. Stephanos. Here, from under the paving of an earlier Byzantine church, Danish archaeologists unearthed in 1904 many extremely important inscriptions including the famous "Chronicle,,, of the temple, a long chronological list of the priests of Athene, etc.

On the north slope of the acropolis looking on the large harbour, at a place called Vigli, there is a very ancient small sanctuary known as "V o u-k o p i o n,,, and situated in a natural recess in the rock. In the centre, there

*Reconstruction of the acropolis of Lindos (after E. Dyggve).*

are the traces of a small temple (9.20 × 4.50 m.) divided into a pronaos and a cella. The foundations are perfunctorily made and the walls consisted probably of sundried bricks. Archaeological findings have shown that it dates back to the Geometric Period (10th to 9th century B.C.) i.e. to the time of Dorian colonization (like the earlier findings of the temple of Athene or the acropolis) and that it continued to be used well into historical times. The name of the sanctuary is connected with a special sacrifice to Athene, known as Voukopia or Theodhaisia; prevented by the prehellenic tradition from sacrificing oxen in the sanctuary of the rock (since Athene would only accept "fireless„ offerings there), but unwilling to give up their familiar sacrificing practices, the Dorians found a compromise solution by removing the place of oxen sacrifice outside the acropolis sanctuary. The many — about 40 — incriptions engraved at various times around the rock, are connected with these sacrifices.

A large round monument of the Classical Period at the end of the promontory closing the large harbour to the north, is locally known as "t h e g r a v e   o f   K l e o b o u l o s„. Its external perimeter measures 28.43 m and it is preserved to a height of approx. 2.80 m. Its main body stands on a somewhat broader base, with regularly hewn blocks and terminating with a slightly projecting cornice; the roof was conical. In the main body of the building, which is entered through a doorway to the NNW, a passage leads to a small funeral chamber (3.87 m. long by 2.34 m. wide); the grave is in the rock forming the floor of the room at the southwestern side. In antiquity the monument was surrounded by an enclosure. In later years it was converted to St. Emilian's church (pl. 64).

## The monuments of the acropolis

The almost triangular rock, which is lower and wider to the north and climbs higher while becoming narrower to the south, is accessible only from the north; the west side is very steep, the east side descends in a perpendicular wall to the sea. Its aspect is now dominated by the walls of the Knights, whereas the ancient walls were much lower and did not conceal the buildings (pl. 55 and fig. on p. 110).

After the first and lowest gateway into the medieval wall, and after the first stairway, there comes a plateau with two impressive ancient monuments carved out of the rock on the right side: a round p l a t f o r m (exedra) and adjacent to it a s h i p in relief (pl. 60). This ship shows only its stern, is 4.76 m. long, and the stem of the stern rises to 5.50 m. (pl. 60). It faithfully reproduces all the details of the craft which was probably of the type known as "triemiolia„ (even the highly ornamented seat of the captain is shown on the r i g h t h a n d edge of the deck); this work provides therefore valuable information concerning the construction of ancient seacraft; but it is also interesting in that it shows the appreciation of those ancient seamen for a lovely ship, and it makes a very fitting pedestal for the statue of a sea-warrior, which indeed it was, because on the largest part of the ship stood the bronze statue of Agesandros; the inscription informs us that : "the Lindians have honoured Agesandros son of Mikion with a gold crown, a statue, and precedence at the games for his virtue and care for the people of Lindos. Made by Pythokritos son of Timocharis of Rhodes„ (for information about the sculptor who must be maker of the ship of the base as well, see p. 45). The historical occasion which induced the making of this valuable work in 180 B.C. is unknown. On the left and by the side of the monument, a round platform carved out of the rock at about the same time, was probably intended as a necessary adjunct to the overall architectural arrangement of the area. In front of this, also carved out of the rock is a low rectangular base of an altar or statue.

Later, in the 3rd or 4th century A.D., the priest of Athene Aglochartos, engraved one of his epigrams on the back support of the platform, at the left side saying that he had planted olive trees on the rock of Athene and comparing his work with the services rendered by the heroes of Attica Keleos and Ikarios:

῾Ως Κελεὸς σταχύεσσι περιβρείθουσαν ἄρουραν
Δηοῖ γειομόρου ἄνθεμα θῆκε βίου·
ὡς αὐτοῦ δώροισιν ἐριστάφυλον Διονύσου
Εἰκάριος ἐρατὴν εὗρε γεωπονίην·
εἴκελον Ἀγλώχαρτος ἀπημάντοισιν ἐλαίαις
στέψιν Ἀθηναίης Λίνδου ὕπερθεν ἄκρην.

A few remains of the ancient stairway to the acropolis are visible lower on the right of the platform and the relief of the ship.

Reaching the upper plateau of the acropolis (pl. 59) by the later stair-

way, we see first on our right the now ruined P a l a c e o f t h e C o m m a n-
d e r of the medieval castle of the Knights (fig. on. p. 110, E) and adjacent
to its south wall, the remainsof S t. J o h n ' s B y z a n t i n e c h u r c h.
But in the front are the remains and the reconstructed columns of the
broad hellenistic Doric Stoa, which constituted a sort of magnificent façade
and front entrance for the entire ancient sanctuary (fig. on p. 110, Γ and
pls. 62-63). It was built farther f r o n t than the ancient propylaeum (fig. on p.
110, B) and its staircase of the 5th century, but had incorporated the staircase.
It has the general shape of a theatre stage (including the two wings), or of
a wide and shallow ⊓ (with a long middle line and two short legs); its total
length is 88 m., the depth 8.90 m. Of the 42 columns of its façade, 8 belong to each of the side wings and the remaining 26 to the main body a-
long the front. Behind this colonnade, the walls of the stoa, upon reaching the older staircase to the propylaeum, form an angle and turn towards
the colonnade framing the staircase. In this way there was no wall behind
the eight middle columns of the façade, and one could see through the interval of the columns the stairway ascending to the propylaeum. This type of
arrangement is unique and should probably be attributed to the then new
hellenistic tendency toward a three-dimensional architectural setting. The
Doric columns were polygonal up to 1/3 of their height, becoming fluted
thereafter. The entire building was 6.20 m. high from the base upward. The
level of the base was reached by a flight of stairs on the north side, opposite the middle of the stoa. From the form of the architectural members
and other archaeological observations, it would seem that the stoa was
built around 200 B.C., at the heyday of Rhodes. It closed monumentally
the front (north) plateau but did not block (esthetically) the way by a
mere straight-lined façade. As the two side wings projected ahead of the
main body, the stoa opened as it were towards the plateau in a dignified
gesture of invitation from the goddess to the world.

Apart from being planted with trees, this s q u a r e was adorned with various smaller monuments, such as the r o u n d p l a t f o r m dedicated by the family of one Pam-
phylidas in 215 B.C. Noteworthy is also a slender, elegantly worked base (1, 23 m. high)
of the 2nd century B.C., terminating above with the imitation of a rock, on which lay a

*Lindos. Reconstruction of the «Large Stoa».*

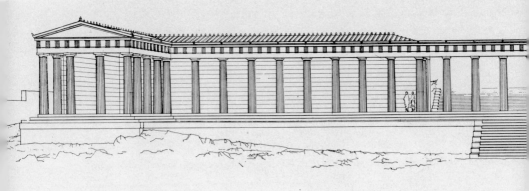

statue of Herakles. At the front, the base has a sculptured altar with a pointed concha and above this an amusing epigram in which the sculptor, Lysias, son of Pyrrandros of Chios, describes the statue and praises his own merits.

Behind the large hellenistic stoa Γ, the much narrower straircase later incorporated into the stoa, led to the p r o p y l a e u m proper (fig. on p. 110, B). The propylaeum and the staircase were built together (the latter upon the remains Z of the archaic staircase of Kleoboulos, see p. 108) immediately after the "Synoecism" of 408 B.C., and are reminiscent of comparable Athenian works. The transverse wall, which constitutes the central part of the structure, has five entrance openings; at the front, rear, left and right there were rooms and stoas. The east and west wings, at right angles with the transverse wall are symmetrical on the façade, where they, too, terminate with a stoa, but behind the transverse wall, the west wing is larger than the east, contains more rooms, and extends to the wall of the ancient acropolis separating the immediate a r e a of the temple from the rest of the site.

To the rear (south), the t e m p l e (fig. on p. 110, A) has preserved its walls fairly well, and recently some of the columns were reconstructed. It was a Doric amphiprostyle tetrastyle structure, i.e. it had columns (4 each) only at the two short sides (front and rear), which is rather rare. It is 22.40 m. long and 7.80 m. wide. From the prodomos, a doorway gave access to the cella, which was closed on the side of the opisthodomos. A projection in the cella, rising above the even level of the floor, was perhaps where the ceremonial statue stood. As attested by the architectural members and other archaeological observations, this temple was built in the 2nd half of the 4th century, in the place, and most probably with the same design as the old temple of Kleobaulos, which had been destroyed by fire in 342 B.C.

Built on the highest point of the rock, the temple formed the terminal of the step-like perspective offered by the stoa and, behind it, the propylaeum, to anyone approaching from the north. The three buildings together — stoa, propylaeum, temple — adapted as they are to the natural shape and axis of the rock, led it an architectural form that seems to express its essence in a pure and perennial manner.

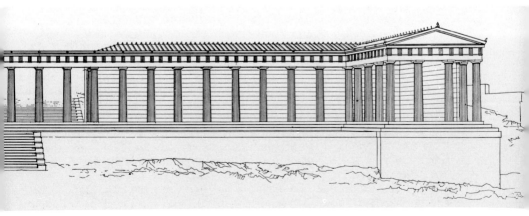

# SUPPLEMENT
## by J.D KONDIS
### FORMER GENERAL
### DIRECTOR OF ANTIQUITIES AND RESTORATIONS

Since this book was first published in 1949, a great deal has been added to our knowledge about the ancient city of Rhodes as described in pages 56-59 and 92-95. Relevant information from the sources has been interpreted and a first attempt has been made to reconstruct the original pattern of the town plan of ancient Rhodes in a general way. Also, the course of the wall surrounding the ancient city has been determined.

All this has been achieved with the help of some earlier discoveries of vestiges of buildings, combined with the recognition that the axes of modern roads which may safely be assumed to have taken the place of ancient roads, have the same general orientation as that suggested by the remains of ancient buildings.

Excavations carried out on the basis of this preliminary study have been continued in the last twenty years. Their results not only confirmed the assumptions of that early study, but brought new corroborating evidence to light, though they have not yet answered all pending questions. This explains why the design (p. 91) shows a more complete diagram of the road axes, but still not the actual layout of the city's road-net.

To present such a layout would indeed be premature and possibly misleading, and might lead investigators to unfounded conclusions.

Even so, the work done so far represents an outstanding achievement if one considers that this is a town which has never ceased being inhabited and therefore subject to continuous change since antiquity, and that most of its area is now occupied by later buildings.

As the representation (p. 91) shows, the ancient city spread over the whole area now occupied by the modern town, except only the northeastern part. In antiquity, this site was occupied by the necropolis which lay outside the fortified walls.

For the most part, the ground covered by the town slopes gently down from the acropolis — the Monte Smith plateau (alt. 80-111m.) — to the sea, which explains the designation of Rhodes by ancient writers as "theatre-like,, (see p. 56-57).

The town's seaside now includes two harbours, the large main harbour and the harbour known as Mandraki (p. 55); both show evidence of ancient

constructions. There is a third harbour east of the main port, at Akandia. This looks now like a natural bay, with only a few visible traces of ancient construction works.

There were two additional harbours in antiquity. One at the seaside corresponding to the present "Hotel of the Roses,, and another to the northwest in Psaropoula. The latter is still being used when the violent south winds make access to the regular harbours impossible. This was the ancient Rhodians' answer to the still not satisfactorily solved problem of harbour facilities.

As mentioned in the book (p. 57), the smaller harbour Mandraki was used by the ancients as an arsenal. Remains of Rhodes' famous ancient shipyards have been discovered all along the coast.

Some of these remain uncovered and can be seen behind the north-western part of the medieval town's wall at a small distance from the harbour, a considerable part of which has been filled with alluvial mud.

The r o a d - n e t of the ancient town was obviously designed to fit a sort of module (an imaginary grid) resulting from the division of its total area into square stadia and subdivisions of square stadia: half-stadia and "hecatontapodiae,, (hundred-foot areas) or "plethra,,. The stadion measure used was based on the foot unit (0.35 times $600 = 201$ m.).

On this pattern, the longitudinal (N-S) and the transverse (E-W) roads were traced, with crossings at regular intervals. All streets were straight and "continuous,, as the ancients described them. The main roads (the "Plateae,, of the ancients) were designed along the sides of the stadia rectangles of the grid pattern, whereas secondary roads followed the half-stadia divisions. The "hecatontapodiae,, were the smallest block units ascertained so far. Where measurements were possible, it has been found that road width ranged from 5 m. to 16 m.

The division of the city area is certain to date back to the time when the city was first built, rather than to any subsequent rearrangement. This is attested to by the fact that all traces of buildings found so far, even the most ancient, fit the pattern. It is also certain that the division was not restricted to the areas where streets were to be built, which again shows that the layout of the road-net was not its sole purpose. This can be seen, for instance, on the acropolis, which was not in fact a stronghold, but simply one, the highest, section of the city.

The a c r o p o l i s was "full of open spaces and groves,,. The pattern is evident in these open spaces or plateaus as well as in the alternating levels and the arrangements of the space in terraces. The situation must have been similar in the main part of the city, where successive terrace patterns are predominant.

The terraced design is probably associated with the ancient space-arrangement concept of Eastern Greeks. In Rhodes, however, its application seems to have been particularly conducive to the admirable unity which, according to all accounts, was a main feature of the city down to the late antiquity (p. 58). In other words, this arrangement helped to implement the classical principle of equal distribution of building blocks.

The whole concept of Rhodes was in fact basically classical. It is interesting to note in this connection that the orientation of the road axes determined by the division of the area was independent from the direction of the geological relief, and that the rhythmical alternation of roads and terraces was adhered to even when expensive earth moving and other technical works were involved. The strongly personal style and the plastic character of the city does not seem to have been affected by later modifications.

The ancient information according to which Rhodes was built by Hippodamos of Miletus (p. 56) relates the city to one of the great milestones of world oekistics. Hippodamos may in fact be regarded as the father of systematic town planning, itself yet another of the many achievements of human civilization which originated in the 5th century.

This open question as to whether Hippodamos actually worked in Rhodes (which is highly probable despite existing objections) or whether the plan of Rhodes was merely a typical example of Hippodamos' art, detracts nothing from the significance of Rhodes in this area. The important point is that while practically nothing is known about the other towns reputedly designed by this great Miletian, Rhodes can provide positive clues to the real contribution of Hippodamos to the development of town planning.

One of the most reliable sources, Aristotle, mentions that Hippodamos first invented "division of towns,,. This passage has been variously construed, and as "division,, is commonly —but incorrectly— identified with r e g u l a r road patterns, i.e. a succession of crossing straight streets, a type of plan known before Hippodamos, the accuracy of Aristotle's testimony has been doubted as regards the term "first,, anyway.

We now find, however, that in Rhodes —considered by the ancients a Hippodameian city— a preliminary d i v i s i o n, based on the stadion and its subdivisions, had certainly been made, and that the subsequent design of the road plan and the arrangement of levels was in accord with that division — as can also be seen from the vertical, altitudinal arrangement.

Having ascertained this, it is difficult to suppose that the term "division,, had in Aristotle's mind any meaning other than its normal one: i.e. the rational division of space by a determined divisor or factor, in this case a subdivision of the stadion. It would seem, then, that what Aristotle (a pedantic sticker to the accurate use of language) meant, was that Hippodamos was the first to introduce a r a t i o into the structure of towns, implying the use of a specific geometric system — most probably the system seen in Rhodes.

It is, besides, very doubtful whether Hippodamos was an architect at all, it would seem rather that his contribution to town building was of a purely geometrical nature. His concern was the division of the town; the road plan too, but this, though simultaneous, was secondary. The actual building was done by others, at some later and not necessarily fixed, time.

About Rhodes, specifically, it has been established that these constructions were not yet complete a hundred year after the foundation of the city.

The fact that some later texts refer to Hippodamos as an architect is probably due to an anachronism, due to the fact that several aspects of town planning had merged in the interval. D i v i s i o n was now of interest only in relation to the road-net plan, and road construction became, along with building construction, the province of the architect. It was natural for the people of these later times, to confuse Hippodamos' geometrical work with the architect's job and thus attribute to him qualifications he did not really possess.

Another activity, closely and inseparably associated with road planning, was "nemesis,, ( = distribution), which meant an advance distribution of the total area of the city into zones, each of which would serve a determined purpose: public building sector, residential area, commercial district, etc. — a system rediscovered by European town planners many centuries later. The location of the important buildings was also determined at this stage. D i s- t r i b u t i o n obviously had to comply with the rules imposed by d i v i- s i o n.

In Rhodes, we were able to see that, in terms of city distribution, the acropolis was the zone set aside for monuments, and this arrangement was dictated by the rules of division. Similar information has been obtained in respect of the area below the acropolis, where gymnastic and similar facilities were discovered.

We have already referred to the utilization of the area of the small harbour for military purposes. Similar areas probably surrounded the other harbours, designed to facilitate harbour operations.

As to the likely location of the "agora,, (market-place), it was probably in the centre of the city and this was surely the position assigned to this function from the beginning, as mentioned in the main text (p. 57); the same is true of the "Deigma,,, the commercial display centre situated near the agora.

In one of the monumental zones, the Rhodians had erected the "Ptolemaion,, which, as we learn from ancient tradition, was flanked on each of its four sides by a stadion-long stoa — another example of division; a block consisting of one large building, covering an area of 1 sq. stadion.

Residential areas existed all over the town with the exception of the acropolis.

Also scattered throughout the town were monumental zones, whose exact extent has not yet been ascertained.

Among the events connected with the history of Rhodes, one of far-reaching effect on the town's development was the destructive earthquake of the year 226 B.C. Most of the buildings had to be renovated thereafter.

It was then also that the fortifications —already old and outdated at the time of the earthquake— were rebuilt. Their inadequacy had become apparent during the siege by Demetrios in 306 B.C., and was a result of the rapid development of siege art which had occurred shortly after the foundation of Rhodes, mainly due to more effective catapults and other machines.

After the earthquake, the fortified walls were added to and renovated to a great extent. The new walls were thicker, and their bulk consisted of large rectangular hewn stones, which increased their resistance to shock. They were also higher to defy the new siege machines. All in all, the new fortifications were so highly adapted to the new requirements, and so solidly built with high-quality craftsmanship, that in the time of Pausanias, four hundred years later, the by then famous fortification of Rhodes was still considered one of the best in the world.

Many important parts of the fortified walls have been excavated, some of them during earlier diggings, but most after the war, based on the preliminary study laid out as a means of shedding light on unanswered questions concerning the city of Rhodes. Some of the older parts of the wall discovered mainly in the northwestern corner of the acropolis illustrate the building method used during the early period which is the so-called "intertwined,, system. The masonry work is not massive; the surfaces are built with regular rectangular blocks, while the core of the wall is filled with smaller, non-bearing stones, and dirt.

The wall enclosed the harbours by following to coastline and extending over the length of the breakwaters. There the construction became mixed — a wall on the outside, wharves on the inside. This can be seen clearly at the southern part of the small harbour.

Most residential building ruins found belong to the period after 226 B.C. Remains of buildings dating from the first period can often be seen beneath the newer houses. Buildings of the Hellenistic Period show evidence of extensive renovations or repairs, while houses built initially during the Roman Period are rare.

This predominance of hellenistic homes, as well as public buildings, is due mainly to the extensive reconstruction undertaken after the earthquake, and to the solid construction which ensured their long life.

Renovations, on the other hand, do not seem to be related with the earthquake alone. Obviously, the earthquake gave the Rhodians an opportunity to satisfy the new living requirements as well as the new "hellenistic,, aesthetic concepts at a time of economic prosperity.

The quality of house construction is largely excellent, the external walls —the façades in particular— being generally built with large rectangular stones, and looking as if they belonged to monumental public buildings rather than to private homes. The inner walls are ornamented with moulded or painted decorations. The floors of the more ambitious rooms were covered with mosaics, some noteworthy samples of which have been found in recent years.

The types of houses, the internal partitions and general details have not yet been identified, because the excavations carried out so far were hurried parts of an official program. Their main purpose was to provide information which would enable the authorities to decide on the fate of a number of plots, whose owners were seeking building permits; all this in the climate of a building rush.

That these difficult investigations carried out under such unfavourable conditions in a fragmentary way, could finally be combined into an organically integrated whole, was due exclusively to the preliminary archaeological study referred to in the beginning of this complement. Unavoidably, however, only the most fundamental problems concerning the position of the plots concerned in the overall plan of the ancient city could be dealt with in the context of the official ·investigation.

The details, no matter how important, had to be left until later, when they could be studied at leisure in the most interesting parts of the town, where no building permits were granted.

So, no integral individual building units or blocks have actually been identified, which might provide a basis for a relevant study. Whatever one said about the houses of Rhodes at present would be based on general impressions and would therefore be premature — and this we do not intend to do.

A few general remarks, however, are in order. All usual ancient house types are represented in Rhodes: houses built around a roofless rectangular inner courtyard, with or without a peristyle; "closed,,, especially "double,, houses i.e. houses consisting of a ground floor and an upper floor. In all residential districts investigated so far, there is a fairly high proportion of large buildings and it can be safely assumed that large buildings dominated the picture.

It is not certain whether this preponderance of large buildings is a hellenistic or earlier characteristic. In the 4th century it was said that the Rhodians built as if they were immortal. It is also unknown if the adjustment of building blocks to the requirements of the prior division of the city was achieved in the same manner in the Classical and in the Hellenistic Period.

However, while d i v i s i o n with its permanent consequences, has certainly served to maintain a balanced general pattern (see p. 58), the hellenistic concept with its marked influence on the eastern Aegean, is sure to have played a role in the final style of the city.

E.g. the better known terraced arrangement in the area between the east side of the acropolis and the gymnastic buildings below is inspired by the hellenistic conception. The "Pergamon,, style seen in the largely reconstructed terraces in this zone is different from that of the terraces in other parts of the city. On the acropolis also, another, almost contradictory, hellenistic tendency can be seen in the, picturesque, slightly reminiscent of clacissism shapes of the "Nymphaea,, hewn out of the rocky subsoil (p. 92-93). Interestingly, both these tendencies are evident also in the sculptural works found now and again in the city and more particularly on the acropolis.

Information about the s a n c t u a r i e s which are discovered or known from ancient sources to have existed in the city is given in the main text (pp. 56 - 59 and 90 - 94). Only new information resulting from subsequent excavations and studies need to be added here.

The location of the t e m p l e o f H e l i o s which has not been discovered so far but is supposed to have stood somewhere in the area of the Castello Hill, was n o t in the "lower acropolis,, (p. 58), for the simple reason that the "lower acropolis,, never existed. Earlier investigators had mistaken some existing terraces supporting walls like those found in other parts of the city, for fortifications, deducing from them the existence of a lower acropolis.

The "A s k l e p e i o n,,, also known from written testimonies, has not been found either (pp. 56-59); but from an inscription studied subsequently, we now have some information concerning its general form. The sanctuary was situated on two successive terraces on the slope looking down on the big harbour, somewhere at the limits of the medieval town, where the descent is steeper. The lower terrace which was flanked by walking stoas like those of the Asklepeion of Cos, was accessible through a propylon. The upper terraces included the temple itself, and other official buildings. The resemblance between this arrangement and the first hellenistic formation of the Asklepeion of Cos, may support the assumption that the Asklepeion of Rhodes served as a model for the Asklepeion of Cos.

As regards the "D i o n y s i o n,, of Rhodes, earlier investigators had assumed that some vestiges found at the northeast wall of the medieval town, west of the temple of Aphrodite, were parts of this Dionysion (p. 58). Excavations carried out during the last war, however, showed that the ruins were part not of a sanctuary but of a m o n u m e n t a l  t e t r a p y l o n. This tetrapylon led from the area of the small harbour to a paved a v e n u e flanked by stoas on either side. Beside this tetrapylon, at a lower level, can be seen the ruins of the shipyards remaining uncovered as stated earlier. When the propylon and the avenue were built some time near the beginning of the 3rd century B.C., the shipyards were no longer in use and they had been covered by earth. The small harbour itself had already been largely filled with mud. The starting point of the new avenue was one of the "plateae,,, with which the city had always been studded from north to south.

This is one of the very few modifications of the Roman Period found in Rhodes. Even this, however, while adding a note of grandeur to the scene, did not depart from the old rules governing the overall plan of the city.

In the excavated residential areas, the Roman Period, as mentioned earlier, is represented mainly by renovations of earlier hellenistic buildings. It would seem that unlike the earthquake of 226 B.C., that of 142 A.D., though destructive enough, did not initiate a period of intensive building activity.

S e w a g e  a n d  w a t e r  s u p p l y  i n s t a l l a t i o n s deserve a brief discussion; these owe technically admirable facilities, and attest to the high economic prosperity of the city. Both the sewage and the water supply systems were installed when Rhodes was first established and added to later.

All drainage canals for rainwater were underground and covered, and followed the course of the roads. The central sewage canals can be seen at strategic points down the slope, usually beneath important thoroughfares. They are rectangular and often as large as 1.85 m. by 1.05 m. with walls built with large rectangular stones; they were covered on top with great flagstones. They show an excellent craftsmanship, hardly inferior to that of public buildings on the surface. The additional canals built in the Hellenistic Period or later are mostly arched or pointed upward.

The layout of the water supply network was not bound to that of the roads. The conduits are of varying shapes; some are built entirely with rectan gular stones, while others are hewn out of the live rock with only some additions of masonry.

The aqueduct was reinforced along its course by means of water tapping installations, which were found, both superficial and underground during excavations. The distribution of water to the various areas of the town was effected by means of clay pipes, found in plenty in the layers of pounded earth which formed the surface of ancient roads.

From the e a r l y C h r i s t i a n P e r i o d, represented by some important monuments in the countryside of Rhodes, there was until recently nothing but a few architectural members, mainly capitals, in the town itself. Some of these capitals were used by way of decorations, when the Castello was rebuilt.

In the last years, the remains of an early Christian basilica were found, though not entirely excavated, in the monumental area below the acropolis of Rhodes. This structure seems interesting. It is estimated to be about 60 m. in length and the fragments of mosaics which covered the floor are of good craftsmanship. A few other walls near this basilica, and contemporary with it, indicate that, as usual, the basilica formed the centre of a cluster of buildings all serving religious purposes.

It is interesting that several architectural members, pedestals, etc. had been found earlier at the same site, suggesting that the Christian church had been preceded by an ancient sanctuary, and one of considerable importance at that.

It is hoped that when the site of the basilica is fully excavated, not only the monuments will come to light, but some important questions regarding the history of the city, e.g. at what time the area outside the medieval wall was abandoned, may be answered as well. During excavations of the residential zones, it was noted that early Christian finds become increasingly scarce, and are so few even before the end of the early Christian period, that they can hardly be regarded as evidence of habitation. It would be instructive in this context to ascertain if this Christian unit had been established and operated within or without the boundaries of the city.

Post-war excavations extended fairly far into the medieval town. The extensive damages by bombing during the last war cleared some areas, making them accessible to investigation. The results of excavations yielded valuable information concerning not only the ancient but also the medieval town of Rhodes.

One interesting conclusion from observations made at the excavations combined with clues provided by buildings preserved in the m e d i e v a l t o w n is that during a long period of time including the whole of the Byzantine Period and the early Period of the Knights, the town developed in accordance with the ancient plan, though of course the rules were not so strictly adhered to as in antiquity.

The important factor in this period was the need to meet the multiple living and defense requirements within the cramped space included in the wall of the great harbour. The ancient plan of the city was thus changed, distorted and mutilated but remained visible nevertheless.

The old form of the town lost its physiognomy to a much greater extent during the shorter but more active — in terms of building activity — Period of the Knights, which started in the last decade but one of the 15th century and ended in 1522, when Rhodes fell to the Turks (p. 61).

During this period, unlike the preceding one, the development of Rhodes was not dictated by chance circumstances. It was directed by architects and craftsmen who may have not worked together, but had the same aesthetic background and the same tendencies.

The great destructions which occurred during the first Turkish siege and the great earthquake of 1481 made it possible for Rhodes to be architecturally renewed, in a way which provided a better context for the remaining old buildings. Basically, however, the new architectural climate was markedly different from, if not hostile to, the classical conception from which the purity of the ancient plan had sprung.

It is not irrelevant in this connection, that of all the "ancient continuous,, thoroughfares, only the "street of the Knights,, survived the new pattern with only slight deviations of its axis; even this was really only due to the fact that its straight course fitted the ceremonial character appropriate to its position as a link between the Roman Catholic cathedral and the administrative and religious centre of the Knights in the Castello. The straight line of the other broad roads became distorted by curves, and repeated interruptions.

If the "magna et communis platea,,, the present Socratous street, has retained so far, within its indefinite limits, the straight course of the ancient roads it has replaced, this is only because the new order was never fully extended to this area.

In spite of everything, the final pattern of the medieval town which has been preserved with only slight modifications to this day, never broke completely away from its ancient roots; except that it now, takes a trained eye to see the connection.

Outside the medieval town, developments took a simpler turn. When the countryside was abandoned, the ancient roads gradually became country lanes or paths and were preserved as such. After the Turkish occupation, when the Greeks were driven out of the walled town and were forced to establish their own settlements, the "marassia,,, on the outside, they quite naturally adopted the existing traces of the ancient road plan. The same thing happened again after the 17th century, when the Aegean became gradually safer, and agglomerations began to form in the part of the ancient town not included within the medieval walls, which became again fully peopled.

Thus Rhodes, besides its outstanding interest in terms of the history of town planning, is also a typical example of a Greek town in the Aegean Sea, bearing the genuine and still alive vestiges of millennia of historical evolution and the recognizable marks of successive civilizations.

Ph. Villiers de l'Isle Adam
1521-1522

Fabrizio del Carretto
1513-1521

Guy de Blanchefort
1512-1513

Aimerie d'Amboise
1505-1512

Pierre d'Aubusson
1476-1505

| | |
|---|---|
| —— Asphalt road | ● Medieval site |
| — Non-asphalt road | ■ Byzantine site |
| ⌃ Airport | ↓ Yacht supply station |
| L Archaeological site | ～ Beach facilities |

# LIST OF EXHIBITS OF THE MUSEUM OF RHODE
## by GR. KONSTANTINOPOULOS
### EPHOR OF ANTIQUITIES

In the courtyard of the Museum there is a hellenistic lion of Lartian stone. The arrangement of exhibits in the two (ground-floor and first floor) galleries has not yet been completed.

**Large patient ward.** Gravestones from the period of the Knights — 14th, 15th and 16th century. Also coats of arms of the Order, of the Great Magisters and of various Knights.

**Refectory of the Knights.** S o u t h e r n   s i d e : Marble fragment with representation. of a hoplites from a Roman tetrapyle. — Votive relief with crowned bull heads. — Small marble slab with inscription; Roman Period : "Priest of Tripolis Minion Dorotheou,,. — Part of sarcophagus of the Late Roman Period with representation of bull head, garland, a male and a female figure.

W e s t e r n   s i d e : Relief with representation of the hero Kakkabos on horseback. — Marble altar from Nissyros; the three figures in relief were added subsequently. — Relief representing sacrifice; figures moving from right to left : child accompanying sacrificial animal; altar; forepart of horse in front. The other sides were also decorated with reliefs. — Two reliefs showing Kakkabos. — In front, small marble funerary urn for bones or ashes with female and male figures in relief, bull heads and garlands.

N o r t h e r n   s i d e : Grave stele with a male and a female figure of the Late Roman Period. — Another similar grave stele with three figures. — Still another with two figures. — Long and narrow stele with two figures, one the figure of a child; all exhibits from Nissyros.

E a s t e r n   s i d e : Grave stele with three figures; from Nissyros. — Inscribed marble stele with pediment and antae; six figures are shown. S o u t h   o f   e n t r a n c e, toward the large hall : Fragment of grave stele with two antae, one with bent figure of dead woman, the other with two figures. — Relief with representation of Kakkabos. — Relief showing hero on horseback holding kantharos and turning toward snake on tree. In front of the horse, an altar and 3 ceremonial figures.

**Timarista room.** Grave stele of Crito and Timarista.

S o u t h e r n   s i d e : Fragment of grave stele of the Classical Period; female figure with raised right arm. — Upper part of male torso, headless; Roman Period. — Above, head of Victory (Nike) with garland — Fragment of circular hellenistic altar, Rhodian type. — Fragment of grave stele, Classical Period, with figure of dead man; little servant boy following. — Relief with female figure, a copy of a relief decoration on the base of the statue of Athene Parthenos by Phidias. — On the pillar of the arch, a small grave stele of the Late Hellenistic Period with inscription reading : "Philomena Antiphilou,,.

W e s t e r n   s i d e : Upper part of seated female figure; excellent sculpture of the 5th c. B.C. — The stele of Crito and Timarista (text page 97, pl. 17).

N o r t h e r n   s i d e : Lower part of grave stele with relief representing boy; period of austere style, around 460 B.C. — Grave stele of Calliarista, of the well-known Attic type of the 4th c. B.C., found in the town of Rhodes. — Head and part of body of large, probably grave, female statue. Found in the town of Rhodes. — Lower part of grave stele with seated figure in relief. Late 5th c.; from Nissyros.

E a s t e r n   s i d e : At the junction of the two arches, grave stele of hoplites. Holds helmet and leans on hellenistic column; from the cemeteries of Rhodes (pl. 18). — Near the window toward the refectory, fragment of marble stele with seated figure. — Opposite the corner formed by the junction of the two arches, a marble acroterium. Below, unadorned marble grave stele with inscription reading "Boulagoras Boulacleus„ ; Hellenistic Period.

**Room of archaic exhibits.** Two marble statues of young men (Kouroi) (pl. 10). — Anthemion of porous stone, probably crowning a grave stele. — Two heads of Kouroi (pl. 11); from Kamiros. — Archaic perirranterion; from Kamiros.

**Room of large Aphrodite** (entrance through the garden door).
N o r t h e r n   s i d e : Marble head of woman; Hellenistic Period. — Lower part of female statue, richly draped. — Fragment of sima with anthemion from the temple of Apollo Erethimios. — Lower part of female figure with vivid movement; richly draped. — Part of male head from marble relief. — Fragment of larger relief representing battle; a kneeling female figure is visible. — Torso of female statue, headless, wearing chiton and himation.— Female head with veil (pl. 22).— Lower part of male figure, "pounded„ : Hellenistic Period. — Portrait-head of a Roman. — Marble male figure, "pounded„ ; Hellenistic Period. — Portrait - head of Antoninus Pius (2nd c. B.C.). — Relief showing Zeus seated in throne. — Exhibited in front of the above is a three-figured "Hecataeum„ ; archaistic type, found on the acropolis of Rhodes. — Headless herma; Hellenistic Period. — Broken head of child.

W e s t e r n   s i d e : Torso of Aphrodite emerging, very "pounded„. — Head of Hermes with inlaid eyeballs, archaic. — Female statue, dressed, very "pounded„ ; Hellenistic Period. — Muse (2nd c. B.C.). — Statue of Aphrodite, probably ceremonial, in the attitude of "Aphrodite Anadyomène„ (emerging). Found in the sea, when the foundations of the "Hotel of the Roses„ were laid.

S o u t h e r n   s i d e : Fragment of relief; Hermes accompanying nymph in front of building. — Statue of nymph, with raised leg resting on rock (pl. 26). — Relief of warrior holding sword in left hand. — Marble head of god Helios (pl. 1). — Relief fragment representing sea battle; one figure at the ship's stern, another in the sea trying to hold on to stern. — Head of athlete (pl. 23). — Headless male torso; Hellenistic Period. — Porous stone brick with representation of sacrifice; at centre, two women leading bull; behind, very "pounded„ Satyr; deities shown on right above.

E a s t e r n   s i d e : Marble head of woman, with strong movement. — Lower part of dressed female figure; Late Hellenistic Period. — Pictorial head of philosopher; Rhodian work of the 1st c. B.C. — Statue of boy dressed with chiton; arms missing.

**Small passageway.** Head of Dionysos, of porphyry stone; 1st c. B.C. — Three fragments from the sima of the temple of Apollo Erethimios (near the village Tholoo of Ialyssia).

**Room of small Aphrodite** (entrance through the western door).

S o u t h e r n   s i d e : In showcases, statuettes of Asclepios and Hygeia; Roman Period (pls. 19, 21). — Statuette of dressed woman in rigidly erect posture. — Nymph, dressed, seating on rock with right foot put forward; Late Hellenistic Period (pl. 25). — Statuette of man, dressed. — Similar statuette with upper part of body partially uncovered. — In showcase, small marble head of woman. — Statuette of Asclepios, "very pounded" (2nd c. B.C.). — In case, small male head. — Small male statue, nude. — Statuette of naked boy holding puppy. — Statuette of dressed woman, Rhodian type. — Fragment of archaic relief showing Hermes accompanying nymph; from Kamiros. — Marble Roman altar with representation of goddess "Potnia theron", fruits and leaves on upper surface.

E a s t e r n   s i d e : Torso of boy, naked to the buttocks. — Relief with female figure, archaistic. — Statue of nymph rising from rock.— Statue of dressed woman; head and arms missing. — Statue of woman, seated, richly clothed; Fortune of Antiochia type. — Headless statue of boy, carrying fruit in chiton. — Statuette of woman; Hellenistic Period.

N o r t h e r n   s i d e : Statue of man, with chlamys thrown back. — Headless statue of dressed woman leaning on left. — Headless statuette of man. — Dressed figure, Rhodian type. — Nude statue of man, headless. — Statue of Artemis, headless. — Fragment of female statue. — Statue of seated Zeus (headless, arms missing), on marble altar; Hellenistic Period. — Statue of woman, dressed. — Statue of Zeus, standing. — Statue of Satyr "pounded"; Middle Hellenistic Period.

W e s t e r n   s i d e : Small herma from Kamiros. — The "Aphrodite of Rhodes" (pl. 24, see also text, p. 101). — Figure of Satyr, fallen upon winebag; Middle Hellenistic Period (2nd c. B.C.).— Statuette of Dionysos; the drunken god leans on wall; a work of the Middle Hellenistic Period, centrifugal composition.

**Small Menandros room.** Statuette of nymph. — Fragment of sima from the temple of Apollo Erethimios. — Small grave relief; young man carrying unidentified object on his palm; small dog near his legs.

E a s t e r n   s i d e : Head of woman; Roman Period. — Statue of young woman, archaistic, excellent craftsmanship; head and arms missing. — Fragment of marble sarcophagus; rider holding horse; Roman Period. — Portrait-head of the comic poet Menander; copy of statue - archetype from the workshop of the sons of Praxiteles. — Statue of Artemis. — Head of woman, poorly preserved. — Fragment of relief with quadriga representation; Victory on other side.

N o r t h e r n   s i d e : Female statue, "pounded". — Grave marble altar with rich decoration, Rhodian type; in front, the dead man on bed; woman standing (1st c. B.C.). — Above : fragment of hellenistic pillar with relief representation of man, dressed. — Female statuette.

W e s t e r n   s i d e :  Portrait-head of a Roman; holes for fastening wreath.— Statue of woman, dressed.— Portrait-head, Roman Period, broken.

**Rooms of vases.** Exhibited here are vases and small objects (grave furnishings-kterismata) from the cemeteries of ancient Ialyssia i.e. from the village of Trianta to Kremasti (pls. 2, 3, 4, 6, 7, 8, 9, 13. 14, 15).

**Room A.** Findings from the 9th to the 6th c. B.C., separated by graves. As a rule at that time the dead were first burnt and then buried with the kterismata remaining after the cremation. Children were not cremated. They were put in large p i t h o i (jars). Two such jars can be seen in showcases in this room.

**Rooms B and Γ.** Findings from the same cemeteries; 6th to 5th c. B.C. In the 3rd room, attic vases : Kylikes, hydriae, and amphorae, mostly black-figured; the very few red-figured vases are of excellent workmanship. The three Rhodian vases in showcases 1, 2, and 3 (Fikelloura type) are characteristic; they show that Rhodian pottery had survived the great boom of the Attic workshops.

**Room Δ.** W e s t e r n   s i d e :  In the first showcase beside the fireplace : Rhodian vases of the Protogeometric and Early Geometric Period. In the other showcases, mainly Attic black-figured vases. Second showcase : on the lower shelf a Rhodian, Fikelloura type, amphora. Third showcase. The Laconic hydria on right above (pl. 15) is noteworthy : duel over a fallen dead warrior. Names of warriors inscribed from right to left : Archilochidas, Deinomachos, Synis. On back: stripe dancers. The shape of the hydria shows influence of bronze craft. Rhodian pyxis (pl. 9) decorated with a row of partridges.

In the last showcase, some fifty kterismata from one grave are displayed.

**Room E.** Attic vases, mostly. In the second showcase a large, but not whole, hydria; a fine amphora and some kylikes, one of very good workmanship. Noteworthy exhibit in the third showcase are the clay masks and the naïve representation of a mourning scene : the dead man on his deathbed, the woman seated on the bed, without connection with the dead man.

**Room ΣT.** In the showcases near the walls, objects from Ialyssos cemeteries (6th, 5th, and 4th c. B.C.). Jewels from the Mycenaean graves of Ialyssos, jewels and small objects from the excavations at the acropolis of Kamiros are temporarily exhibited in this room; they include a necklace made of a multitude of spherical glass beads. In the third showcase, silver Rhodian coins found during recent excavations in Rhodes.

Exhibited on the  n o r t h e r n   s i d e  of the Museum are vases and kterismata from Kamiros.

**Room Z.** Early vases, protogeometric and geometric, from various parts of the excavations carried out in settlement of Kamiros.

**Room H.** Objects from the 7th and 6th c. B.C., mostly Rhodian oinochoae decorated with alternating stripes of floral and animal designs.

— The rearrangement of Kamiros vases is continued in the other rooms.

# BIBLIOGRAPHY

GENERAL AND SPECIAL TEXTS

E. B i l i o t t i - a b b é C o t t r e t, L'ìle de Rhodes 1881.

S k e v o s   Z e r v o s, Rhodes capitale du Dodécanèse, Paris 1920

A. M a i u r i, Rodi, "Il picolo cicerone,,, 1921

G. J a c o p i, Rodi, Bergamo 1933.

H. v a n   G e l d e r, Geschichte der alten Rhodier, Haag 1900

H i l l e r   v o n   G ä r t r i n g e n, article Rhodos in Real-Enzyklopädie der klass. Altertumswissenschaft (Pauly-Wissowa-Kroll) Supplementband V, pp. 731ff (both are fundamental texts on ancient history; nothing similar exists in respect of medieval and modern history)

T r. E v a n g e l i d i s : Rhodiaka, Rhodos, 1917 (miscellaneous but unprocessed material concerning medieval and modern history). Abundant material published in the periodical Annuario della Scuola Archeologica di Atene and in the periodicals of the former historical-archaeological institute of Rhodes: Clara Rhodos Vol. I-X and Memorie Vol. II-III.

G. J a c o p i, Lo Spedale dei Cavallieri e il Museo archeologico di Rodi, Roma 132

C h r. B l i n k e n b e r g-K.F. K i n c h, Lindos, Fouilles et recherches 1902-1914, Vol. I (the small votive offerings, 1931) - II (the inscriptions, 1941) - III Le Sanctuaire d' Athena Lindia et l'architecture lindienne (E. Dyggve) - Catalogues des Sculptures trouvées sur l' acropole (V. Poulsen) 1960.

B e r n a r d   R o t t i e r s, Monuments de Rhodes, Vol. I-II, Bruxells 1828 /30

A. G a b r i e l, La cité de Rhodes, Vol. I-II, Paris, 1921 /23 (a fundamental work on the period of the Knights)

A. K. O r l a n d o s, La maison paysanne dans l'ìle de Rhodes in the periodical L' Hellenisme contemporain, Mai-Juin 1947 pp. 223 ff. Concerning early Christian relics and Byzantine and post-Byzantine monuments of Rhodes see a study by the same author in the periodiccal "Arch. of the Byzantine  Monuments of Greece,, Vol. 6 (1948)

I. D. K o n d i s, Recent Restoration and Preservation of the Monuments of the Knights in Rhodes, B.S.A. 47, 1952, p. 213.
—A contribution to the study of the town plan of Rhodes, Rhodos 1954
—Zum antiken Stadtbauplan von Rhodos, AM 73, 1958, p. 146

G r. C o n s t a n t i n o p o u l o s : The Rhodian World I. Lindos. A contribution to the study of the history of Lindos prior to the Synoecism, Athens 1972.

J e a n   C u r r i e, Rhodos und die Inseln des Dodekanes, Stuttgart 1972

H a t t o   H. S c h m i d t, Rom und Rhodes. Geschichte ihrer politischer Beziehungen seit der ersten Berührung usw (1957. Münchner Beiträge zur Papyrus Forschung und Reschtsgeschichte C. H. Beck).

Z e e r   G o l d m a n n, The Hospice of the Knights of St. John in Akko in Archaeology 19, 1966, pp. 182-198.
For results of excavations from 1950 onwards, see ΠΑΕ 1951-1960, ῎Εργον 1954 1961 and ΑΔ 16 (1960) - 25 (1970) Chronika.
[The natural morphology, the history, the alphabet, the economic, social and intellectual history of ancient Rhodes, as well as all the disturbed modern history, the monuments, even folklore and development of the Church and of the Greek schools down to the incorporation of the island into Greece (1947) are described in the excellently documented, highly valuable recent book, written in admirable demotic by former high school principal Ch. I. Papaehristodoulou: "History of Rhodes,, (ed. Stegi Grammaton-Technon Dodeconissou,,, Athens 1972, 668 pages) The references at the end of the book are also very useful].
Additional bibliography in articles "Rhodos,, of  Great Greek Encyclopedia and "Rodi,, in Enciclopedia Italiana.

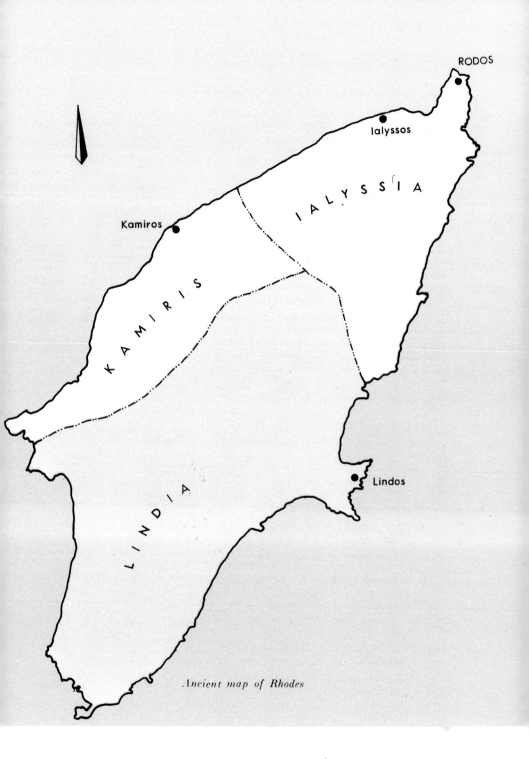

*Ancient map of Rhodes*

## LEGEND TO THE TOPOGRAPHICAL PLAN

**1.** *Inn of the Tonque of Auvergne* **2.** *Historical-archaeological institute* **3.** *Our Lady of the Castle, formerly Enteroum-mosque or Kantouri (the description on page 63 refers to the older form of this building; recently, the Turkish prostoon and the minaret were removent, restoring the original form of the church).* **4.** *Inn of the Tonque of England* **5.** *Hospital of the Knights (Museum)* **6.** *Inn of the Tonque of Italy* **7.** *Unidentified palace* **8.** *Unidentified palace* **9.** *Inn of the Tonque of France* **10.** *Appendage to the above* **11.** *St. Demetrios-Dionysion* **12.** *Chapel with iconostasis* **13.** *Cappelania* **14.** *Inn of the Tonque of Provence* **15.** *Inn of Spain* **16.** *Old St. John's* **17.** *Palace of Great Magister* **18.** *Gate of Cannons* **19.** *Gunpost of the Olives* **20.** *«Castellania»* **21.** *Souleiman mosque* **22.** *Hourmali-medresse* **23.** *Sandri-Tzelepi.* **24.** *St. George's Gate* **25.** *Takedzi mosque* **26.** *Sultan-Moustapha mosque and Souleiman's bath.* **27.** *Abdoul-Tzelil mosque* **28.** *Bab-u-Mestoud mosque* **29.** *Alemnak mosque* **30.** *Retzep-Pasha mosque* **31.** *Peial-el-din mosque* **32.** *Demirli mosque (the description on page 75 refers to the condition of the building up to World War II; it was destroyed by bombing during the war and lies now in ruins).* **33.** *Ibrahim-pasha mosque* **34.** *Houdai mosque* **35.** *Koskinou or St. John's Gate* **36.** *Dolapli-mosque* **37.** *Ilh Mihrab* **38.** *Our Lady of Victory (St. Marie de la Victoire)* **39.** *Gate of the Mills (St. Catherine's)* **40.** *St. Catherine's Hospital* **41.** *Sainte Marie du Bourg* **42.** *Yeni-mosque* **43.** *Admiralty Palace (Metropolitan).*

Πόρτα
D'Amboise

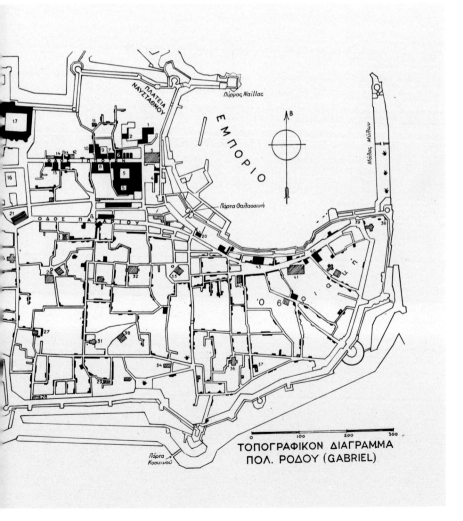

ΤΟΠΟΓΡΑΦΙΚΟΝ ΔΙΑΓΡΑΜΜΑ
ΠΟΛ. ΡΟΔΟΥ (GABRIEL)

**1**

Μαρμάρινο κεφάλι τοῦ θεοῦ Ἡλίου *(2ος αἰ. π.X.)*
Marble head of God Helios *(2nd c. B.C.)*
Marmorkopf des Sonnengottes *(2. Jh. v. Chr.)*
Marmorhuvud föreställande guden Helios *(2 årh. f. Kr.)*

**2**

Ροδιακὴ οἰνοχόη (7ος αἰ. π.Χ.)
*Rhodian oinochoe (wine - vessel)* (7th c. B.C.)
*Rhodische Oinochoe (7. Jh. v. Chr.)*
*Rhodisk oinochoe—vinkrus—(7 årh. f. Kr.)*

**3**

Ἀγγεῖο τύπου «Φικελλούρας» (6ος αἰ. π.Χ.)
*Vase of the «Phikelloura» type (6th c. B.C.)*
*Vase des «Fikellura»- Stils (6. Jh. v. Chr.)*
*Kärl av Fikelluratyp (6 årh. f. Kr.)*

**4**

Κρατήρας (ὕστερα ἀπὸ τὰ μέσα τοῦ 8ου αἰ. π.Χ.)
*Crater (2nd half of the 8th c. B.C.)*
*Krater (nach Mitte des 8. Jh. v. Chr.)*
*Krater — vinblandningskärl — (senare hälf-
ten av 8 årh. f. Kr.)*

**5**

*Χάλκινος πετεινὸς (6ος αἰ. π.X.)*
*Bronze cock (6th c. B.C.)*
*Hahn aus Bronze (6. Jh. v. Chr.)*
*Bronstupp (6 årh. f. Kr.)*

**6-7**

*'Αγγεῖα τύπου «Φικελλούρας» (6ος αἰ. π.X.)*
*Vases of the «Phikelloura» type (6th c. B.C.)*
*Vasen des «Fikellura» - Stils (6. Jh. v. Chr.)*
*Kärl av Fikelluratyp (6 årh. f. Kr.)*

Ἀγγεῖα τύπου «Φικελλούρας» (6ος αἰ. π.Χ.)
ases of the «Phikelloura» type (6th c. B.C.)
asen des «Fikellura» - Stils (6. Jh. v. Chr.)
Kärl av Fikelluratyp (6 årh. f. Kr.)

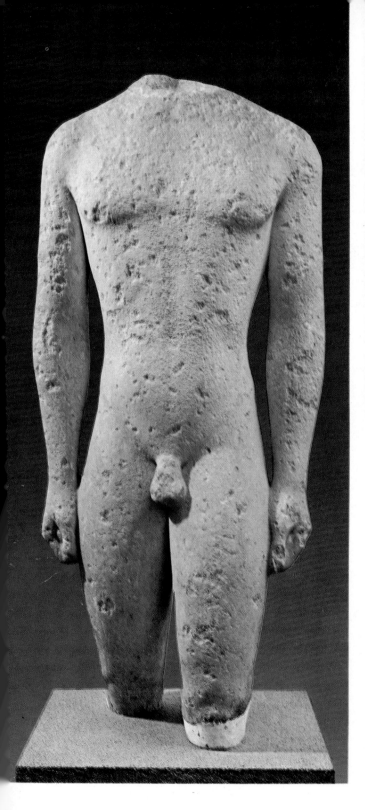

**10**

Κορμὸς κούρου ἀπὸ τὴν Κάμιρο
(β′ μισὸ 6ου αἰ. π.Χ.)
Torso of a Kouros from Kamiros (2nd half of the 6th c. B.C.,
Torso eines Kouren aus Kamiros
(2. Hälfte des 6. Jh. v. Chr.)
Koros från Kamiros (andra häl
ften av 6 årh. f. Kr.)

**11**

Κεφάλι καθημένου ἀγάλματος ἀπ
τὴν Κάμιρο (6ος αἰ. π.Χ.)
Head of a seated statue from Ka
miros (6th c. B.C.)
Kopf einer sitzenden Statue a
Kamiros (6. Jh. v. Chr.)
Huvud av sittande staty från Ka
miros (6 årh. f. Kr.)

## 12

*Πήλινη γυναικεία προτομὴ (α΄ μισὸ 5ου αἰ. π.Χ.)*
*Clay bust of a woman (1st half of the 5th c. B.C.)*
*Weibliche Tonbüste (1. Hälfte des 5. Jh. v. Chr.)*
*Kvinnobyst av terracotta (första hälften av 5 årh. f. Kr.)*

13

'Αττικὸς ἀμφορέας
(β' μισὸ 6ου αἰ. π.Χ.)
Attic amphora
(2nd half of the 6th c. B.C.)
Attische Amphore
(2. Hälfte des 6. Jh. v. Chr.)
Attisk amfora
(andra hälften av 6 årh. f. Kr.)

15

Λακωνικὴ ὑδρία (6ος αἰ. π.Χ.)
Laconic hydria (pitcher) (6 th c. B.C.)
Lakonische Hydria (6. Jh. v. Chr.)
Hydria — vattenkanna —
från Lakonien (6 årh. f. Kr.)

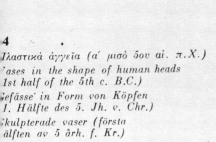

**4**

Πλαστικὰ ἀγγεῖα (α΄ μισὸ 5ου αἰ. π.X.)
*Vases in the shape of human heads
(1st half of the 5th c. B.C.)*
*Gefässe in Form von Köpfen
(1. Hälfte des 5. Jh. v. Chr.)*
*Skulpterade vaser (första
hälften av 5 årh. f. Kr.)*

**16**

'Επιτύμβια στήλη (α' μισό 4ου αἰ. π.Χ.)
Grave stele (1st half of the 4th c. B.C.)
Grabstele (1. Hälfte des 4. Jh. v. Chr.)
Gravstele (första hälften av 4 årh. f. Kr.)

**17**

'Επιτύμβια στήλη τῆς Κριτῶς καὶ Τιμαρίστας (τέλος 5ου αἰ. π.Χ.)
Grave stele of Crito and Timarista (late 5th c. B.C.)
Grabstele der Krito und Timarista (Ende des 5. Jh. v. Chr.)
Gravstele över Krito och Timarista (slutet av 5 årh. f. Kr.)

'Επιτύμβια στήλη πολεμιστοῦ (2ος αἰ. π.Χ.)
Grave stele of a warrior (2nd c. B.C.)
Grabstele eines Kriegers (2. Jh. v. Chr.)
Gravstele över krigare (2 årh. f. Kr.)

Ἄγαλμα Διονύσου (2ος αἰ. π.Χ.)
Statue of Dionysos (2nd c. B.C.)
Statue des Dionysos (2. Jh. v. Chr.)
Staty föreställande Dionysos (2 årh. f. Kr

**20**

Ἀγαλμάτιο Ἀσκληπιοῦ
ῥωμαϊκῆς ἐποχῆς

Roman statuette of Ascle-
pios

Statuette des Asklepios
(römische Epoche)

Statyett föreställande Asklepios från romersk tid

**21**

Ἀγαλμάτιο Ὑγείας ῥωμαϊ-
κῆς ἐποχῆς

Roman statuette of Hygieia

Statuette der Hegäa (römische Epoche)

Statyett föreställande Hygeia från romersk tid

**22**

*Κεφάλι γυναίκας ἀπὸ ἐπιτύμβιο ἄγαλμα (β΄ μισὸ 4ου αἰ. π.Χ.)*
*Head of a woman from a grave statue (2nd half of the 4th c. B.C.)*
*Kopf einer Frau von einem Grabdenkmal (2. Hälfte des 4. Jh. v. Chr.)*
*Kvinnohuvud från gravskulptur (andra hälften av 4 årh. f. Kr.)*

Κεφάλι ἀθλητῆ (β΄ μισὸ 4ου αἰ. π.Χ.)         Kopf eines Athleten (2. Hälfte des 4. Jh. v. Chr.)
Head of an athlete (2nd half of the 4th c. B.C.)    Huvud av atlet (andra hälften av 4 årh. f. Kr.)

**24**

'Η «'Αφροδίτη τῆς Ρόδου» (1ος αἰ. π.Χ.)
The «Aphrodite of Rhodes» (1st c. B.C.)
Die «Aphrodite von Rhodos» (1. Jh. v. Chr.)
Afrodite från Rhodos (1 årh. f. Kr.)

**25-26**

'Αγάλματα Νυμφῶν (α' μισὸ 1ου αἰ. π.Χ.)
Statues of Nymphae (1st half of the 1st c. B.C.)
Statuen von Nymphen (1. Hälfte des 1. Jh. v. Chr.)
Statyer av nymfer (första hälften av 1 årh. f. Kr.)

**27-28**

Ἀεροφωτογραφία τῆς πόλης τῆς Ρόδου
*Aerial view of the town of Rhodes*
*Luftaufnahme von Rhodos*
*Flygfotografi över staden Rhodos*

**29**

῎Αποψη τοῦ Καστέλλο καὶ τῆς ἀγορᾶς (Μαντράκι)
View of the Castello and the market-place (Mandraki)
Ansicht des Kastells und des Marktes (Mandraki)
Vy över kastellet och saluhallen (Mandraki)

**30**

Τὸ Διοικητήριο        Die Präfektur
The Governor's residence    Guvernörspalatset

**31**

Οἱ μεσαιωνικοὶ ἀνεμόμυλοι στὸ Μαντράκι
The medieval wind - mills at Mandraki
Die mittelalterlichen Windmühlen in Mandraki
Mandrakis medeltida kvarnar

**32**
*Πλατεῖα τοῦ Ναυστάθμου*
*The Arsenal Square*
*Platz des Kriegshafens*
*Amiralitetsplatsen*
**33**
*Τὸ Ἀρχαιολογικὸ Ἰνστιτοῦτο*
*The Archaeological Institute*
*Das Archäologische Institut*
*Arkeologiska Institutet*
**34**
*Τὸ Νοσοκομεῖο τῶν Ἱπποτῶν (Ἀρχ. Μουσεῖο)*
*The Hospital of the Knights (Arch. Museum)*
*Das Hospital der Ordensritter (Archäologisches Museum)*
*Riddarsjukhuset — numera arkeologiska museet*

**38**
*Βυζαντινὴ ἐκκλησία*
*A Byzantine church*
*Byzantinische Kirche*
*Bysantinsk kyrka*

**39**
*Βρύση Τουρκοκρατίας*
*A fountain from the period of the Turkish occupation*
*Brunnen aus der Türkenzeit*
*Fontän från turktiden*

**40** Ἡ ὁδὸς Ἁγίου Φανουρίου (παλιὰ πόλη)   *Die Strasse des Hl. Fanourios (Altstadt)*
*The street of St. Phanourios (old town)   Fanoúriosgatan*

**1-43**

ὸ παλάτι τοῦ μεγάλου Μαγίστρου
he palace of the Great Magister
er Grossmeisterpalast
ormästarpalatset

**44**

'Η πόρτα τοῦ Λιμανιοῦ *(Μαρίνα)*
*The Gate to the harbour (Marina)*
*Das Tor im Hafen (Marina)*
*Marinaporten*

**45**

Τὰ ἐρείπια τοῦ ναοῦ τῆς 'Αφροδίτης
*The ruins of the temple of Aphrodite*
*Die Ruinen des Tempels der Aphrodite*
*Ruinerna av Afroditetemplet*

**46**

'Η πόρτα τοῦ "Αη - Γιάννη
*St. John's Gate*
*Das St. Johannes Tor*
*St. Johannes port*

**47**

*Τὸ ἀρχαῖο στάδιο καὶ τὸ θέατρο τῆς Ρόδου*
*The ancient Stadium and the Theatre of Rhodes*
*Das antike Stadion und das Theater von Rhodos*
*Den antika stadion och teatern på Rhodos*

**48**

*Ὁ ναὸς τοῦ Πυθίου Ἀπόλλωνος*
*The temple of Apollo Pythios*
*Der Tempel des pythischen Apoll*
*Tempel helgat åt den pytiske Apollon*

**49**

*Γενική ἄποψη τῆς Καμίρου*
*General view of Kamiros*
*Allgemeine Ansicht von Kamiros*
*Översiktsvy över Kamiros*

**50-52**

*Ἰαλυσός (Φιλέρημος) : 50. Δωρικὴ κρήνη.*
*'51. Ὁ δρόμος γιὰ τὸ Μοναστήρι.*
*52. Ἐρείπια τοῦ ἀρχαίου ναοῦ*
*τῆς Ἰαλυσίας Ἀθηνᾶς.*

*Ialysos (Philerimos): 50. Doric fountain.*
*51. The way to the Monastery.*
*52. Ruins of the ancient temple*
*of Athene Ialysia*

*Ialyssos (Philerimos): 50. Dorischer*
*Brunnen. 51. Die Strasse zum*

*Kloster. 52. Ruinen des antiken Tempels*
*der Athena - Ialysia*

*Ialysos (Filerimos): 50. Dorisk källa.*
*51. Vägen till Monastiri. 52. Ruinerna*
*av Athena Ialysiatemplet*

**3-54**

Ἡ κοιλάδα μὲ τὶς πετα-
ρῦδες

The valley with the butter-
ies

Das Schmetterlingstal

järilsdalen

**55-56**
Ἀπόψεις τῆς Λίνδου
*Different aspects of Lindos*
*Ansichten von Lindos*
*Vyer från Lindos*
**57**
Σπίτι τῆς Λίνδου
*A house in Lindos*
*Haus in Lindos*
*Hus i Lindos*

**58**
Ἄποψις τῆς Λίνδου
Aspect of Lindos
Ansicht von Lindos
Vy från Lindos

**59**
Λίνδος : ἡ ἄνοδος στὸ κάστρο
Lindos : the way leading
up to the Castle
Lindos : Der Aufstieg zur Burg
Lindos : Trappan upp mot borgen

**60**
Λίνδος : ἀνάγλυφο καραβιοῦ
Lindos : ship in relief
Lindos : Relief eines Schiffes
Lindos : Fartygsrelief

**61**

'Ο βράχος τῆς Λίνδου καὶ πά-
νω ὁ ναὸς τῆς 'Αθηνᾶς

The Rock of Lindos with the
temple of Athene on it

Der Felsen von Lindos und
auf dem Gipfel der Tempel
der Athena Lindia

Lindosklippan med Athenatemplet

**62-63**

Τμῆμα τῆς στοᾶς καὶ ἡ με-
γάλη σκάλα

Part of the stoa and the great
stairway

Teil der Säulenhalle und die
grosse Treppe

Del av kolonnaden och den stora
trappan

**54**

Λίνδος: Ο «τάφος τοῦ Κλεο-
βούλου»

Lindos: «The Grave of Kleoboulos»

Lindos: «Grab des Kleobulos»

Lindos: «Kleobulos grav»

**65**

Τὸ λιμάνι τοῦ Ἀποστόλου
Παύλου

The port of Saint Paul

Der Hafen des Apostel Paulus

Aposteln Paulus' sjö

66 Τριάντα: ξυλόγλυπτο τέμπλο  
    *Trianta: wooden carved iconostasis*  
    *Trianta: Holzgeschnitzte Altarwand*  
    *Trianda: Ikonostas med träsniderier*

67 Μουσεῖο λαϊκῆς κοσμητικῆς Ρόδου  
    *The museum of Rhodian popular decorative ar*  
    *Volkskundemuseum Rhodos*  
    *Etnografiska museet på Rhodos*